You are being saved from burning forever, pl
seriously.

Jesus the Christ loves you and has called you.
John 15:19
19 If ye were of the world, the world would love his own: but because ye are not of the world, but I have chosen you out of the world, therefore the world hateth you.

Being with God the Father, Jesus the Christ and the Holy Spirit, on there terms. Please read all of this booklet, for the best life for you.

    Some of the sins (Wrong doing) that if you are doing, you need to turn away from and ask God for forgiveness in Jesus name, Idolatry - Putting anything or person in the place of God the Father the creator, abortion, lesbianism Romans 1:26, Matthew 18:6-8, homosexuality Romans 1:27, Matthew 18:6-8, adultery, masturbation, fighting and doing illegal drugs. Note: Matthew 18:6-8 applies to anyone that causes others to sin.

    God the Father's ten commandment's. Exodus 20:1-17 I am the Lord your God. You shall worship no other gods beside me. You shall not carry God*s name in vain. Remember the Sabbath day to keep it holy. Honor your father and mother. You shall not murder. You shall not commit adultery. You shall not steal. You shall not bear false witness against your neighbor. You shall not covet your neighbor*s house: you shall not covet your neighbor*s wife * Or anything that is your neighbor*s.
The Good news is that Jesus the Christ died for your sins and was raised back to life by God the Father so that you can live forever with them, this booklet tells you how.

God loves mankind, Satan hates mankind, Be on Gods side.

This book is meant to give people a better understanding of the Holy

Bible, hopefully it will become required reading in every church and school, It has been a work of love.

Read some and then reflect on what is said or talk about what you read in Bible study, Then read some more.

This book is not to be recorded. For reasons I will not go into, It is better for everyone this way, Again I say this book is never to be recorded, please respect my decision on this matter, This is also God the Father your creator, will.

If some one is reckless enough to record this book, Please throw the recordings away, Again: This is also God the Father your creator, will.

This book is not to be changed, because it might loss some of its meaning. This is also God the Father your creator, will.

God the Father has given me permission to change this.

I talked to God the Father and he told me to tell people that its ok to record my book, all I ask is that you please record all of it, not just some of it.

What Jesus the Christ says about peace.
John 16:33
33 These things I have spoken unto you, that in me ye might have peace. In the world ye shall have tribulation: but be of good cheer; I have overcome the world.
Having the peace of God.
Philippians 4:6-8
6 Be careful for nothing; but in every thing by prayer and supplication with thanksgiving let your requests be made known unto God.
7 And the peace of God, which passeth all understanding, shall keep your hearts and minds through Christ Jesus.
8 Finally, brethren, whatsoever things are true, whatsoever things are

honest, whatsoever things are just, whatsoever things are pure, whatsoever things are lovely, whatsoever things are of good report; if there be any virtue, and if there be any praise, think on these things.

Note: No matter what happens, read this booklet, do not let the devil (satan) cheat you out of your everlasting life. Do not be condemned to burn forever with the devil.

If you left, for any reason, Even if the reason is me, return back to Jesus the Christ and be healed in every way.

Living a loving life is the answer. Live your loving life.

There is only salvation in God the Father son Jesus the Christ (The sent one).

Repenting of sins.   Saving others is saving yourself.
James 5:19-20
19 My brothers and sisters, if one of you should wander from the truth and someone should bring that person back,
20 remember this: Whoever turns a sinner from the error of their way will save them from death and cover over a multitude of sins.

Note: If you come across any of my books that do not warn you about the devil, throw them away, Thank you.

Philippians 4:8
8 Finally, brothers and sisters, whatever is true, whatever is noble, whatever is right, whatever is pure, whatever is lovely, whatever is admirable if anything is excellent or praiseworthy—think about such things.

Colossians 3:12
12 Therefore, as God's chosen people, holy and dearly loved, clothe

yourselves with compassion, kindness, humility, gentleness and patience. Living a loving life is the answer. Live your loving life.

Pray that people return to God the Father, Jesus Christ and the Holy Spirit.

The prayer.
God the Father, please guide the people back to you Jesus Christ and the Holy Spirit if they left, This I humbly ask in Jesus the Christ Holy name, Amen.

If you would like a hard copy of this booklet tittled: Urgent, Need to know information, For Christians and non Christians.   Please go to amazon.com

Philippians 4:8
8 Finally, brothers and sisters, whatever is true, whatever is noble, whatever is right, whatever is pure, whatever is lovely, whatever is admirable if anything is excellent or praiseworthy—think about such things.
==========
Section - 1 - What happens to Christians.
==========
Section - 2 - Confession of faith, get baptized.
==========
Section - 3 - In the family of God the Father.
==========
Section - 4 - Warning's about your enemy the devil, (satan).
==========
Section - 5 - Listing of sins, that if you are doing, you need to confess and turn away from, if you fail to turn away from that or those sins, try again, and if you keep failing keep trying, do not give up.
==========
Section - 6 - Love yourself enough, to not stop your christen life of love,

do not give up, remember loving others is loving yourself.
==========

Section - 7 - Look to God the Father Son, Jesus the Christ, just like I am, to be saved, Because there is only salvation through him.
==========

Section - 8 - Build or continue your relation with God the Father, Jesus the Christ, The Holy Sprit and the saints.
==========

Section - 9 - Diffarent subjects to study, to help you understand the Holy Bible more.
==========

Section - 10 - Some warnings to be aware of.
==========

Section - 11 - Forgiveness for blasphemy of the Holy Ghost.

This added section is good news, to the Jewish people and everyone else, a lot of people would not be saved if it was not for this provision in the Holy Bible.
==========

Note: Before you start your study remember it is all about love, God the Father, Jesus the Christ and the Holy Spirit love for mankind, mankind kind love for each other.

God the Father love.
St John 3:16-18
16 For God so loved the world, that he gave his only begotten Son, that whosoever believeth in him should not perish, but have everlasting life.
17 For God sent not his Son into the world to condemn the world; but that the world through him might be saved.
18 He that believeth on him is not condemned: but he that believeth not is condemned already, because he hath not believed in the name of the only begotten Son of God.

    Some of the sins (Wrong doing) that if you are doing, you need to turn away from and ask God for forgiveness in Jesus name, some sins are, Idolatry - Putting anything or person in the place of God the Father the creator, murder, abortion, lesbianism Romans 1:26, homosexuality Romans 1:27, adultery, masturbation, fighting and doing illegal drugs. Note: Matthew 18:6-8 applies to anyone that causes others to sin.

Ten Commandments in order, Exodus 20:1-17
   I am the Lord your God.   You shall worship no other gods beside me.   You shall not carry God's name in vain.   Remember the Sabbath day to keep it holy.   Honor your father and mother.   You shall not murder.   You shall not commit adultery.   You shall not steal.   You shall not bear false witness against your neighbor.   You shall not covet your neighbor's house: you shall not covet your neighbor's wife … Or anything that is your neighbor's.

God loves mankind, Satan hates mankind, Be on Gods side.

What Jesus says about fighting and revenge.
Matthew 5:38-39
38 "You have heard that it was said, 'Eye for eye, and tooth for tooth.'
39 But I tell you, do not resist an evil person. If anyone slaps you on the right cheek, turn to them the other cheek also.

Romans 12:19 Do not take revenge, my dear friends, but leave room for God's wrath, for it is written: "It is mine to avenge; I will repay," says the Lord.

Loving others is loving yourself.
Matthew 25:31-46
31 When the Son of man shall come in his glory, and all the holy angels with him, then shall he sit upon the throne of his glory:
32 And before him shall be gathered all nations: and he shall separate them one from another, as a shepherd divideth his sheep from the goats:

33 And he shall set the sheep on his right hand, but the goats on the left.
34 Then shall the King say unto them on his right hand, Come, ye blessed of my Father, inherit the kingdom prepared for you from the foundation of the world:
35 For I was an hungred, and ye gave me meat: I was thirsty, and ye gave me drink: I was a stranger, and ye took me in:
36 Naked, and ye clothed me: I was sick, and ye visited me: I was in prison, and ye came unto me.
37 Then shall the righteous answer him, saying, Lord, when saw we thee an hungred, and fed thee? or thirsty, and gave thee drink?
38 When saw we thee a stranger, and took thee in? or naked, and clothed thee?
39 Or when saw we thee sick, or in prison, and came unto thee?
40 And the King shall answer and say unto them, Verily I say unto you, Inasmuch as ye have done it unto one of the least of these my brethren, ye have done it unto me.
41 Then shall he say also unto them on the left hand, Depart from me, ye cursed, into everlasting fire, prepared for the devil and his angels:
42 For I was an hungred, and ye gave me no meat: I was thirsty, and ye gave me no drink:
43 I was a stranger, and ye took me not in: naked, and ye clothed me not: sick, and in prison, and ye visited me not.
44 Then shall they also answer him, saying, Lord, when saw we thee an hungred, or athirst, or a stranger, or naked, or sick, or in prison, and did not minister unto thee?
45 Then shall he answer them, saying, Verily I say unto you, Inasmuch as ye did it not to one of the least of these, ye did it not to me.
46 And these shall go away into everlasting punishment: but the righteous into life eternal.

===========

Section - 1 - What happens to Christians.

===========

    My advice to you, Is, Come to Jesus the Christ while you still can and live your life of love while you still can because if you do not, you will burn forever in a lake of fire and brimstone.

All that is being said here is believe in God the Father's son Jesus the Christ and try to live a sinless life, love one another and you will be saved.

Romans 8:1-2
1 There is therefore now no condemnation to them which are in Christ Jesus, who walk not after the flesh, but after the Spirit.
2 For the law of the Spirit of life in Christ Jesus hath made me free from the law of sin and death.

Do somthing for Jesus the Christ, Live your life of love, Love for God the Father, Jesus the Christ, Holy Spirit, yourself and your fellowman.

What happens to all Christian's, this scripture is the foundation of the Christian faith, please do something to show your love for God the Father, Jesus the Christ, the saints, your fellow men and yourself.

some examples is: giving money in church, give as much or as little as you want because God the Father loves a cheerful giver, volunteering with a charity or help them financially or do both, etc

1 Corinthians 3:11-15
11 For other foundation can no man lay than that is laid, which is Jesus Christ.
12 Now if any man build upon this foundation gold, silver, precious stones, wood, hay, stubble;
13 Every man's work shall be made manifest: for the day shall declare it, because it shall be revealed by fire; and the fire shall try every man's work of what sort it is.
14 If any man's work abide which he hath built thereupon, he shall receive a reward.
15 If any man's work shall be burned, he shall suffer loss: but he himself shall be saved; yet so as by fire.   Christian's will remain safely and

peacefully with God the Father, Jesus the Christ, The Holy Spirit and the saved one's, Forever, Amen.

You are holy.
1 Corinthians 3:16-17
16 Know ye not that ye are the temple of God, and that the Spirit of God dwelleth in you?
17 If any man defile the temple of God, him shall God destroy; for the temple of God is holy, which temple ye are.
Return or come back to Jesus the Christ and be healed in every way. Living a loving life is the answer, Live your loving life.

    The prayer that people return to God the Father Jesus the Christ and the Holy Spirit if they left.

I ask that you say this prayer.
God the Father Please guide the people back to you Jesus the Christ and the Holy Spirit if they left, This I humbly ask in Jesus the Christ Holy name, Amen.

Scriptual bases.
The healing, Showing Jesus answer requests. Matthew 8:13
13 And Jesus said unto the centurion, Go thy way; and as thou hast believed, so be it done unto thee. And his servant was healed in the selfsame hour. What so ever ye ask in Jesus name, shall be done.

Mark 11:23-25
23 For verily I say unto you, That whosoever shall say unto this mountain, Be thou removed, and be thou cast into the sea; and shall not doubt in his heart, but shall believe that those things which he saith shall come to pass; he shall have whatsoever he saith.
24 Therefore I say unto you, What things soever ye desire, when ye pray, believe that ye receive them, and ye shall have them.
25 And when ye stand praying, forgive, if ye have ought against any: that

your Father also which is in heaven may forgive you your trespasses.

Another example of comming back to God the Father in some of this parable Jesus tells.
Luke 15:20-32
20 And he arose, and came to his father. But when he was yet a great way off, his father saw him, and had compassion, and ran, and fell on his neck, and kissed him.
21 And the son said unto him, Father, I have sinned against heaven, and in thy sight, and am no more worthy to be called thy son.
22 But the father said to his servants, Bring forth the best robe, and put it on him; and put a ring on his hand, and shoes on his feet:
23 And bring hither the fatted calf, and kill it; and let us eat, and be merry:
24 For this my son was dead, and is alive again; he was lost, and is found. And they began to be merry.
25 Now his elder son was in the field: and as he came and drew nigh to the house, he heard musick and dancing.
26 And he called one of the servants, and asked what these things meant.
27 And he said unto him, Thy brother is come; and thy father hath killed the fatted calf, because he hath received him safe and sound.
28 And he was angry, and would not go in: therefore came his father out, and intreated him.
29 And he answering said to his father, Lo, these many years do I serve thee, neither transgressed I at any time thy commandment: and yet thou never gavest me a kid, that I might make merry with my friends:
30 But as soon as this thy son was come, which hath devoured thy living with harlots, thou hast killed for him the fatted calf.
31 And he said unto him, Son, thou art ever with me, and all that I have is thine.
32 It was meet that we should make merry, and be glad: for this thy brother was dead, and is alive again; and was lost, and is found.

If you see something repeated in this book, it is because that is the way, God the Father had me put this book together.

===========
Section - 2 - Confession of faith, get baptized.
===========

Confession of Faith - If you haven't accepted Jesus or if you need to come back to Jesus say these word's: Jesus I believe that You are the Son of God, Jesus I believe that You came down here to earth as a man, Jesus I believe that You died for my sins (Wrong doings) and all of mankind sins, I believe that God Your Father raised You up from the dead and Jesus I believe that You went up into Heaven to be with Your Father, So that we can be forgiven of our sins, Jesus I confess that You are Lord and God and Jesus please forgive me of my sins and accept me into your family, Jesus I believe that You are coming back again for me one day. Amen.

Find a church and get baptized.

Find a church that agree with this document.
Share your faith with your fellowmen by encouraging them to become a Christian and tell them about this website.

===========
section - 3 - In the family of God the Father.
===========

"Being in the Family of God the Father."

Note: The big "G" in God is referring to God the Father and the little "g" in god is referring to every Christian even Jesus the Christ our Brother.

The Spirit of God is the Holy Ghost.
Joel 2:28
28 And it shall come to pass afterward, that I will pour out my spirit upon all flesh; and your sons and your daughters shall prophesy, your old men shall dream dreams, your young men shall see visions:

Romans 8:14-16
14 For as many as are led by the Spirit of God, they are the sons of God.

15 For ye have not received the spirit of bondage again to fear; but ye have received the Spirit of adoption, whereby we cry, Abba, Father.
16 The Spirit itself beareth witness with our spirit, that we are the children of God:

Romans 5:5
5 And hope maketh not ashamed; because the love of God is shed abroad in our hearts by the Holy Ghost which is given unto us.
All of God's Children are part of God and part of Man.

(God the Father) - (Jesus the Christ - the First Born Son of God the Father) - (The Holy Spirit - our Comforter) - (Say your name here because we are also God the Father sons and daughters)

We are included because we are God the Father's Children.

We will always be part of God and part of Man with the Holy Ghost as our comforter.

The Holy Ghost within us is what makes us part of God and part of Man.

Remember Jesus is the first born Son of God (The first to be risen from the dead by God) and we are his brother's and his sister's and we are all God's Children.

While Jesus was on the earth He was part of God and part of Man and he still is.

What made Him that way is found in Luke 1:35
Luke 1:35
35 And the angel answered and said unto her, The Holy Ghost shall come upon thee, and the power of the Highest shall overshadow thee: therefore also that holy thing which shall be born of thee shall be called the Son of God.

Because the Holy Ghost is within Jesus and because Mary berthed him, Jesus is forever part of God and part of Man.

To prove this, After Jesus was risen from the dead he appeared to his disciples being part of God and part of Man, Doing miracles.

Jesus appearing part of God and part of Man.
Luke 24:36-40
36 And as they thus spake, Jesus himself stood in the midst of them, and saith unto them, Peace be unto you.
37 But they were terrified and affrighted, and supposed that they had seen a spirit.
38 And he said unto them, Why are ye troubled? and why do thoughts arise in your hearts?
39 Behold my hands and my feet, that it is I myself: handle me, and see; for a spirit hath not flesh and bones, as ye see me have.
40 And when he had thus spoken, he shewed them his hands and his feet.

Jesus Doing miracles.
St John 21:4-6
4 But when the morning was now come, Jesus stood on the shore: but the disciples knew not that it was Jesus.
5 Then Jesus saith unto them, Children, have ye any meat? They answered him, No.
6 And he said unto them, Cast the net on the right side of the ship, and ye shall find. They cast therefore, and now they were not able to draw it for the multitude of fishes.

The reason Jesus is called the Son of Man is because Mary birthed Him. How we become a child of God the Father is by becoming a Christian.

This is accomplished by believing upon Jesus the Christ and saying this statement : Jesus I believe that You are the Son of God, Jesus I believe that you were born from a virgin woman, Jesus I believe that You died for my sins and all of mankind sins, Jesus I confess that You are Lord and I believe that God Your Father raised You up from the dead and Jesus I believe that You went up into Heaven to be with Your Father Jesus I believe that You are coming back again for me one day, Amen

Next is to get baptized and to receive the Holy Ghost. So again if you have not been baptized, please do so.

The Holy Ghost Is what makes us part of God and because we were born of a woman we are also part of Man.

Jesus the Christ tried to tell people That they also are part of God and part of Man and they almost stoned him for it.

St John 10:22-39
22 And it was at Jerusalem the feast of the dedication, and it was winter.
23 And Jesus walked in the temple in Solomon's porch.
24 Then came the Jews round about him, and said unto him, How long dost thou make us to doubt? If thou be the Christ, tell us plainly.
25 Jesus answered them, I told you, and ye believed not: the works that I do in my Father's name, they bear witness of me.
26 But ye believe not, because ye are not of my sheep, as I said unto you.
27 My sheep hear my voice, and I know them, and they follow me:
28 And I give unto them eternal life; and they shall never perish, neither shall any man pluck them out of my hand.
29 My Father, which gave them me, is greater than all; and no man is able to pluck them out of my Father's hand.
30 I and my Father are one.Note: Jesus is saying that God is with him.
31 Then the Jews took up stones again to stone him.
32 Jesus answered them, Many good works have I shewed you from my Father; for which of those works do ye stone me?
33 The Jews answered him, saying, For a good work we stone thee not; but for blasphemy; and because that thou, being a man, makest thyself God.

34 Jesus answered them, Is it not written in your law, I said, Ye are gods?Note: Jesus is saying to the People that they also are Gods Children (part of God and part of Man).
35 If he called them gods, unto whom the word of God came, and the scripture cannot be broken;
36 Say ye of him, whom the Father hath sanctified, and sent into the world, Thou blasphemest; because I said, I am the Son of God?
37 If I do not the works of my Father, believe me not.
38 But if I do, though ye believe not me, believe the works: that ye may know, and believe, that the Father is in me, and I in him.

Note: Again Jesus is saying that God is with him.

39 Therefore they sought again to take him: but he escaped out of their hand,
Jesus demonstrated some or all of the gifts of the Holy Ghost which proves he has the Holy Ghost and that he is part of God and part of Man.

About the gifts.
1 Corinthians 12:1-11
1 Now concerning spiritual gifts, brethren, I would not have you ignorant.
2 Ye know that ye were Gentiles, carried away unto these dumb idols, even as ye were led.
3 Wherefore I give you to understand, that no man speaking by the Spirit of God calleth Jesus accursed: and that no man can say that Jesus is the Lord, but by the Holy Ghost.
4 Now there are diversities of gifts, but the same Spirit.
5 And there are differences of administrations, but the same Lord.
6 And there are diversities of operations, but it is the same God which worketh all in all.
7 But the manifestation of the Spirit is given to every man to profit withal.
8 For to one is given by the Spirit the word of wisdom; to another the word of knowledge by the same Spirit;
9 To another faith by the same Spirit; to another the gifts of healing by the

same Spirit;

10 To another the working of miracles; to another prophecy; to another discerning of spirits; to another divers kinds of tongues; to another the of tongues:

11 But all these worketh that one and the selfsame Spirit, dividing to every man severally as he will.

Note: I encourage you to find out the gift or gifts you have and use them, Just as Jesus did.
Jesus Said
St John 14:12
12 Verily, verily, I say unto you, He that believeth on me, the works that I do shall he do also; and greater works than these shall he do; because I go unto my Father.

You may ask - well What about where God called Jesus God with a capital "G", and where it says Jesus sits on Gods Throne with God ?.

Remember God with a capital "G" is referring to God the Father.

Jesus being called God with a capital "G".
Hebrews 1:8
8 But unto the Son he saith, Thy throne, O God, is for ever and ever: a sceptre of righteousness is the sceptre of thy kingdom.

Sharing Jesus throne, Jesus sharing Gods throne.
Revelations 3:21
21 To him that overcometh will I grant to sit with me in my throne, even as I also overcame, and am set down with my Father in his throne.

Just like Jesus shared Gods throne, We shall share Jesus throne.
God was sharing his throne with his son Jesus the Christ when he said "O God" with a capital "G", God may not share his throne with us, But we do know that we shall share Jesus throne if we qualify to receive eternal life.

Jesus still remain Jesus the Christ whenever he share's God the Father's throne just as we remain ourselves if we are saved and share Jesus the Christ throne.

I think one of the reasons God shared his throne with Jesus is because he was glad to have his son with him and remember God and Jesus created the heavens and the earth and everything in it together and Jesus worked with God to save mankind from destruction, All we have to do to be saved is believe on Jesus the Christ and live a life of love.

So even though we may not qualify to share Gods throne we do qualify to share Jesus throne if we receive eternal life.

I encourage you to strive to live such a life as to qualify to receive eternal life and to share Jesus the Christ throne.

Remember God is our Father and Jesus is our Brother and we all are one big family.

Note: I have heard people say that Jesus was beaten to the point that a person could not recognize him when he was crucified, This is not true, To prove this, his disciples recognized him when he appeared to them after God rose him up from the dead.

Jesus appearing part of God and part of Man.
Luke 24:36-40
36 And as they thus spake, Jesus himself stood in the midst of them, and saith unto them, Peace be unto you.
37 But they were terrified and affrighted, and supposed that they had seen a spirit.
38 And he said unto them, Why are ye troubled? and why do thoughts arise in your hearts?
39 Behold my hands and my feet, that it is I myself: handle me, and see;

for a spirit hath not flesh and bones, as ye see me have.
40 And when he had thus spoken, he shewed them his hands and his feet.
===========

section - 4 - Warning's about your enemy the devil, (satan).   Understand this, the devil is real. Do not doubt this. He wants to see you burn forever with him. try not to let this happen. There is only salvation in Jesus the Christ. Come to Jesus, God the Father son, if you have not.
===========

    Scripture's about your enemy the devil and how much he hate's you and how much God the Father, Jesus the Christ and the Holy Spirit loves you,
----
2 Timothy 2:26
26 and that they will come to their senses and escape from the trap of the devil, who has taken them captive to do his will.

    One of the tools the devil uses, Is to play mind games with you to get you to hurt yourself or somebody else, DO NOT FALL FOR IT, I fell for one of his lies, and I hope no one was hurt permanently, If anyone was hurt, I already prayed for a swift recovery for that person and I already asked God the Father for forgiveness, In Jesus the Christ Holy name and I believe I am forgiven, I am continuing my Christian journey of love, You can also ask God for forgiveness and continue your journey of love, Remember, Loving other's is loving yourself.

What happened, is I would not talk to this man on the bus, I was on, about my booklet.

    God love's you and will work with you for a good out come, Just like he love's me and is working with me for a good out come.

If you feel that you failed God the Father, Jesus the Christ and the Holy Spirit in a big way, Don't worry, Stay with them anyway and believe and serve them anyway, For we all should strive for perfection, God the Father, Jesus the Christ and the Holy Spirit already won the battle against the devil

also known as satan, angel of light, day star, roaring lion, lucifer, these are some of his name's.

Looking to God the Father and Jesus the Christ and the Holy Spirit and the warning Jesus tells us about the devil.

1 Peter 5:6-11

6 Humble yourselves therefore under the mighty hand of God, that he may exalt you in due time:

7 Casting all your care upon him; for he careth for you.

8 Be sober, be vigilant; because your adversary the devil, as a roaring lion, walketh about, seeking whom he may devour:

9 Whom resist stedfast in the faith, knowing that the same afflictions are accomplished in your brethren that are in the world.

10 But the God of all grace, who hath called us unto his eternal glory by Christ Jesus, after that ye have suffered a while, make you perfect, stablish, strengthen, settle you.11 To him be glory and dominion for ever and ever. Amen.

Ephesian 6:11-18 Put on the whole armour of God.

11 Put on the whole armour of God, that ye may be able to stand against the wiles of the devil.

12 For we wrestle not against flesh and blood, but against principalities, against powers, against the rulers of the darkness of this world, against spiritual wickedness in high places.

13 Wherefore take unto you the whole armour of God, that ye may be able to withstand in the evil day, and having done all, to stand.

14 Stand therefore, having your loins girt about with truth, and having on the breastplate of righteousness;

15 And your feet shod with the preparation of the gospel of peace;

16 Above all, taking the shield of faith, wherewith ye shall be able to quench all the fiery darts of the wicked.

17 And take the helmet of salvation, and the sword of the Spirit, which is the word of God:

18 Praying always with all prayer and supplication in the Spirit, and

watching thereunto with all perseverance and supplication for all saints;s.

Jesus is the only way to salvation, he destroys the works of the devil,
John 10:9-11

9 I am the door: by me if any man enter in, he shall be saved, and shall go in and out, and find pasture.

10 The thief cometh not, but for to steal, and to kill, and to destroy: I am come that they might have life, and that they might have it more abundantly.

11 I am the good shepherd: the good shepherd giveth his life for the sheep.and now he forever live's

----

Be righteous
1 John 3:7-9

7 Little children, let no man deceive you: he that doeth righteousness is righteous, even as he is righteous.

8 He that committeth sin is of the devil; for the devil sinneth from the beginning. For this purpose the Son of God was manifested, that he might destroy the works of the devil.

9 Whosoever is born of God doth not commit sin; for his seed remaineth in him: and he cannot sin, because he is born of God.

Resist the devil and he will flee.
James 4:7

7Submit yourselves therefore to God. Resist the devil, and he will flee from you.

Again: One of the tools the devil uses, Is to play mind games with you to get you to hurt yourself or somebody else, DO NOT FALL FOR IT, I fell for one of his lies, and I hope no one was hurt permanently, If anyone was hurt, I already prayed for a swift recovery for that person and I already asked God the Father for forgiveness, In Jesus the Christ Holy name and I believe I am forgiven, I am continuing my Christian journey of love, You can also ask God for forgiveness and continue your journey of love,

Remember, Loving other's is loving yourself.

What happened, is I would not talk to this man on the bus, I was on, about my booklet.

God love's you and will work with you for a good out come, Just like he love's me and is working with me for a good out come.

If you feel that you failed God the Father, Jesus the Christ and the Holy Spirit in a big way, Don't worry, Stay with them anyway and believe and serve them anyway, For we all should strive for perfection, God the Father, Jesus the Christ and the Holy Spirit already won the battle against the devil also known as satan.

One of the things the devil (Gods enemy) does is try to make you think that things are more worse than they really are, and it's just not.

The devil's fate.
Revelation 20:10
10 And the devil that deceived them was cast into the lake of fire and brimstone, where the beast and the false prophet are, and shall be tormented day and night for ever and ever.

This is the end of my warnings about the devil (satan),your enemy.

==========

section - 5 - Listing of sins, that if you are doing, you need to confess and turn away from, if you fail to turn away from that or those sins, try again, and if you keep failing keep trying, do not give up.

==========

Beware of pride - It is often considered the opposite of shame or of humility.

Beware of vanity - Being to proud of yourself or your achievements, Vanity is an enemy of the Spirit and must be constantly brought to the cross and crucified.

Try to stay humble - Understanding the biblical meaning of "humble" is essential for anyone seeking to deepen their faith and practice. It invites us to reflect on our attitudes, challenge our pride, and embrace a lifestyle rooted in servanthood and love. As we strive to embody humility, we align ourselves with the teachings of Jesus and the heart of God, ultimately leading to a more fulfilling and purposeful spiritual journey.

God the Father hates sins so much, he destroyed every one on the planet, except, eight people in the great flood, consider this as you read.

Genesis 6:11-13
11 The earth also was corrupt before God, and the earth was filled with violence.
12 And God looked upon the earth, and, behold, it was corrupt; for all flesh had corrupted his way upon the earth.
13 And God said unto Noah, The end of all flesh is come before me; for the earth is filled with violence through them; and, behold, I will destroy them with the earth.

Repenting of sins.   Saving others is saving yourself.
James 5:19-20
19 My brothers and sisters, if one of you should wander from the truth and someone should bring that person back,
20 remember this: Whoever turns a sinner from the error of their way will save them from death and cover over a multitude of sins.

Try to live a sinless life. If you fail, try again. We all should strive for perfection, even if we fall short of it sometimes.

The eyes is the key to the body and we should be careful about what we see.
Matthew 6:21-23
21 For where your treasure is, there your heart will be also.

22 The eye is the lamp of the body. If your eyes are healthy, your whole body will be full of light.
23 But if your eyes are unhealthy, your whole body will be full of darkness. If then the light within you is darkness, how great is that darkness!
Matthew 5:29
29 And if thy right eye offend thee, pluck it out, and cast it from thee: for it is profitable for thee that one of thy members should perish, and not that thy whole body should be cast into hell.

1 Corinthians 6:18-20
18 Flee from sexual immorality. All other sins a person commits are outside the body, but whoever sins sexually, sins against their own body.
19 Do you not know that your bodies are temples of the Holy Spirit, who is in you, whom you have received from God? You are not your own;
20 you were bought at a price. Therefore honor God with your bodies.   All that is being said here is believe in God the Father's son Jesus the Christ and try to live a sinless life, love one another and you will be saved.

   I strongly ask that you stop watching television shows and movies, throw out your DVDs, and try to be careful of the music you listen to and the books you read.   they can send a worldly message.   Meaning: They promote all kinds of sins. Do this for your own good   Remember the Holy Spirit of God the Father is doing it right alone with you, what ever you are doing, try not to grieve it.

If you discover that you are grieving the Holy Spirit, stop what you are doing and ask for forgiveness.

I am stressing this point to you because it is very important, God the Father, Jesus the Christ, the Holy Spirit and the saints, hates sins and they expect for us to hate sins as well.

There is a strong possibility that you might get severely punished by God the Father for watching television shows and movies and playing video games promoting all sorts of sins it, throw out your DVDs and video games, and try to be careful of the music you listen to and the books you read, Take this seriously.

If it starts to change your morals, for the worse, stop it, This is all about cleaning yourself up for yourself and your creators.

There is also the possibility that you may or may not get demon oppressed by watching certain movies, television shows, reading books, and playing video games or playing certain music with all sorts of sins in excess. Please leave those things alone, for your own good. Do something positive with your time.

Check out this website about stop watching television.
Top 10 Reasons You Should Stop Watching TV -
https://personalexcellence.co/blog/stop-watching-tv/

The prayer: God the Father, please free me from any demon that may tempt me or oppress me, this I humbly ask in Jesus Christ Holy name. Amen.

If God the Father frees you, try not to go back into what you were doing. Keep trying until you are free. Do not give up. If you are sinning, you need to confess and ask God the Father for forgiveness and turn away from those sins; if you fail to turn away from those sins, try again and if you keep failing, keep trying. Do not give up.

A list of the sins (Wrong doing) that if you are doing, you need to turn away from and ask God for forgiveness in Jesus name, some sins are, Idolatry - Putting anything or person in the place of God the Father the creator, murder, abortion, lesbianism Romans 1:26, homosexuality Romans 1:27, adultery, masturbation, fighting and doing illegal drugs.

God the Father, ten Commandments in order,
Exodus 20:1-17   I am the Lord your God.   You shall worship no other gods beside me.   You shall not carry God's name in vain.   Remember the Sabbath day to keep it holy.   Honor your father and mother.   You shall not murder.   You shall not commit adultery.   You shall not steal.   You shall not bear false witness against your neighbor.   You shall not covet your neighbor's house: you shall not covet your neighbor's wife Or anything that is your neighbor's.

Note: To the churches and schools. Post, read, pass out copies to church members and to the public and talk about these sins and the ten commandments, often.

God loves mankind, Satan hates mankind, Be on Gods side.

What Jesus says about fighting and revenge.
Matthew 5:38-39
38 You have heard that it was said, Eye for eye, and tooth for tooth.
39 But I tell you, do not resist an evil person. If anyone slaps you on the right cheek, turn to them the other cheek also.

About revenge.
Romans 12:19
19 Do not take revenge, my dear friends, but leave room for God's wrath, for it is written: It is mine to avenge; I will repay, says the Lord.
==========

section - 6 - Love yourself enough, to not stop your christen life of love, do not give up, remember loving others is loving yourself.
==========

Love yourself enough, to not stop your christen life of love, do not give up, remember loving others is loving yourself.

Matthew 25:31-46

31 When the Son of man shall come in his glory, and all the holy angels with him, then shall he sit upon the throne of his glory:
32 And before him shall be gathered all nations: and he shall separate them one from another, as a shepherd divideth his sheep from the goats:
33 And he shall set the sheep on his right hand, but the goats on the left.
34 Then shall the King say unto them on his right hand, Come, ye blessed of my Father, inherit the kingdom prepared for you from the foundation of the world:
35 For I was an hungred, and ye gave me meat: I was thirsty, and ye gave me drink: I was a stranger, and ye took me in:
36 Naked, and ye clothed me: I was sick, and ye visited me: I was in prison, and ye came unto me.
37 Then shall the righteous answer him, saying, Lord, when saw we thee an hungred, and fed thee? or thirsty, and gave thee drink?
38 When saw we thee a stranger, and took thee in? or naked, and clothed thee?
39 Or when saw we thee sick, or in prison, and came unto thee?
40 And the King shall answer and say unto them, Verily I say unto you, Inasmuch as ye have done it unto one of the least of these my brethren, ye have done it unto me.
41 Then shall he say also unto them on the left hand, Depart from me, ye cursed, into everlasting fire, prepared for the devil and his angels:
42 For I was an hungred, and ye gave me no meat: I was thirsty, and ye gave me no drink:
43 I was a stranger, and ye took me not in: naked, and ye clothed me not: sick, and in prison, and ye visited me not.
44 Then shall they also answer him, saying, Lord, when saw we thee an hungred, or athirst, or a stranger, or naked, or sick, or in prison, and did not minister unto thee?
45 Then shall he answer them, saying, Verily I say unto you, Inasmuch as ye did it not to one of the least of these, ye did it not to me.
46 And these shall go away into everlasting punishment: but the righteous

into life eternal.

Endure unto the end.

Luke 21:7-19

7 And they asked him, saying, Master, but when shall these things be? and what sign will there be when these things shall come to pass?

8 And he said, Take heed that ye be not deceived: for many shall come in my name, saying, I am Christ; and the time draweth near: go ye not therefore after them.

9 But when ye shall hear of wars and commotions, be not terrified: for these things must first come to pass; but the end is not by and by.

10 Then said he unto them, Nation shall rise against nation, and kingdom against kingdom:

11 And great earthquakes shall be in divers places, and famines, and pestilences; and fearful sights and great signs shall there be from heaven.

12 But before all these, they shall lay their hands on you, and persecute you, delivering you up to the synagogues, and into prisons, being brought before kings and rulers for my name's sake.

13 And it shall turn to you for a testimony.

14 Settle it therefore in your hearts, not to meditate before what ye shall answer:

15 For I will give you a mouth and wisdom, which all your adversaries shall not be able to gainsay nor resist.

16 And ye shall be betrayed both by parents, and brethren, and kinsfolks, and friends; and some of you shall they cause to be put to death.

17 And ye shall be hated of all men for my name's sake.

18 But there shall not an hair of your head perish.

19 In your patience possess ye your souls.

===========

section - 7 - Look to God the Father Son, Jesus the Christ, just like I am, to be saved, Because there is only salvation through him.

===========

Look to God the Father son, Jesus the Christ, just like I am, to be saved, Because there is only salvation through him.

Jesus say's.
John 14:6
6 Jesus saith unto him, I am the way, the truth, and the life: no man cometh unto the Father, but by me.
==========

section - 8 - Build or continue your relation with God the Father, Jesus the Christ, The Holy Sprit and the saints.
==========

Build or continue your relation with God the Father, Jesus the Christ, The Holy Sprit and the saints.
Matthew 22:36-40
36 Master, which is the great commandment in the law?
37 Jesus said unto him, Thou shalt love the Lord thy God with all thy heart, and with all thy soul, and with all thy mind.
38 This is the first and great commandment.
39 And the second is like unto it, Thou shalt love thy neighbour as thyself.
40 On these two commandments hang all the law and the prophets.

If you love the lord your God with all your heart and with all your soul, and with all your mind and if you love your neighbor as yourself you will not want to do anything against God, and also you will not want to do anything against your neighbor, This is how we fulfill the law.

That is why Jesus said in (Matthew 22:40) On these two commandments hang all the law and the prophets.

And also in (Galations 5:14) further confirms Jesus statement.
14 For all the law is fulfilled in one word, even in this; Thou shalt love thy neighbour as thyself
==========

section - 9 - Diffarent subjects to study, to help you understand the Holy Bible more.
==========

The Person of Christ.
Colossians 1:15-23
15 Who is the image of the invisible God, the firstborn of every creature:
16 For by him were all things created, that are in heaven, and that are in earth, visible and invisible, whether they be thrones, or dominions, or principalities, or powers: all things were created by him, and for him:
17 And he is before all things, and by him all things consist.
18 And he is the head of the body, the church: who is the beginning, the firstborn from the dead; that in all things he might have the preeminence.
19 For it pleased the Father that in him should all fulness dwell;
20 And, having made peace through the blood of his cross, by him to reconcile all things unto himself; by him, I say, whether they be things in earth, or things in heaven.
21 And you, that were sometime alienated and enemies in your mind by wicked works, yet now hath he reconciled
22 In the body of his flesh through death, to present you holy and unblameable and unreproveable in his sight:
23 If ye continue in the faith grounded and settled, and be not moved away from the hope of the gospel, which ye have heard, and which was preached to every creature which is under heaven; whereof I Paul am made a minister;

Ephesians 1:3-14
3 Blessed be the God and Father of our Lord Jesus Christ, who hath blessed us with all spiritual blessings in heavenly places in Christ:
4 According as he hath chosen us in him before the foundation of the world, that we should be holy and without blame before him in love:
5 Having predestinated us unto the adoption of children by Jesus Christ to himself, according to the good pleasure of his will,
6 To the praise of the glory of his grace, wherein he hath made us accepted in the beloved.
7 In whom we have redemption through his blood, the forgiveness of sins, according to the riches of his grace;
8 Wherein he hath abounded toward us in all wisdom and prudence;

9 Having made known unto us the mystery of his will, according to his good pleasure which he hath purposed in himself:

10 That in the dispensation of the fulness of times he might gather together in one all things in Christ, both which are in heaven, and which are on earth; even in him:

11 In whom also we have obtained an inheritance, being predestinated according to the purpose of him who worketh all things after the counsel of his own will:

12 That we should be to the praise of his glory, who first trusted in Christ.

13 In whom ye also trusted, after that ye heard the word of truth, the gospel of your salvation: in whom also after that ye believed, ye were sealed with that holy Spirit of promise,

14 Which is the earnest of our inheritance until the redemption of the purchased possession, unto the praise of his glory.

Romans 8:28-31

28 And we know that all things work together for good to them that love God, to them who are the called according to his purpose.

29 For whom he did foreknow, he also did predestinate to be conformed to the image of his Son, that he might be the firstborn among many brethren.

30 Moreover whom he did predestinate, them he also called: and whom he called, them he also justified: and whom he justified, them he also glorified.

31 What shall we then say to these things? If God be for us, who can be against us?

Question: Who are the predestinated, Called, Justified and Glorified. Answer: The answer is found in (St John 3:16-18) - (Romans 10:9-13)

John 3:16-18

16 For God so loved the world, that he gave his only begotten Son, that whosoever believeth in him should not perish, but have everlasting life.

17 For God sent not his Son into the world to condemn the world; but that

the world through him might be saved.

18 He that believeth on him is not condemned: but he that believeth not is condemned already, because he hath not believed in the name of the only begotten Son of God.

Romans 10:9-13

9 That if thou shalt confess with thy mouth the Lord Jesus, and shalt believe in thine heart that God hath raised him from the dead, thou shalt be saved.

10 For with the heart man believeth unto righteousness; and with the mouth confession is made unto salvation.

11 For the scripture saith, Whosoever believeth on him shall not be ashamed.

12 For there is no difference between the Jew and the Greek: for the same Lord over all is rich unto all that call upon him.

13 For whosoever shall call upon the name of the Lord shall be saved.

----

1 John 1:5-10

5 This then is the message which we have heard of him, and declare unto you, that God is light, and in him is no darkness at all.

6 If we say that we have fellowship with him, and walk in darkness, we lie, and do not the truth:

7 But if we walk in the light, as he is in the light, we have fellowship one with another, and the blood of Jesus Christ his Son cleanseth us from all sin.

8 If we say that we have no sin, we deceive ourselves, and the truth is not in us.

9 If we confess our sins, he is faithful and just to forgive us our sins, and to cleanse us from all unrighteousness.

10 If we say that we have not sinned, we make him a liar, and his word is not in us.

THE PRAYER FOR FORGIVENESS

Father God in heaven. Even though I strive to live a sin free life, I know I probably have not.

Please forgive me any sins that I have done. This I humbly ask in Jesus Holy name, Amen.

Ephesians 2:4-10

4 But God, who is rich in mercy, for his great love wherewith he loved us,
5 Even when we were dead in sins, hath quickened us together with Christ, (by grace ye are saved;)
6 And hath raised us up together, and made us sit together in heavenly places in Christ Jesus:
7 That in the ages to come he might shew the exceeding riches of his grace in his kindness toward us through Christ Jesus.
8 For by grace are ye saved through faith; and that not of yourselves: it is the gift of God:
9 Not of works, lest any man should boast.
10 For we are his workmanship, created in Christ Jesus unto good works, which God hath before ordained that we should walk in them.

Right with God
Romans 5:1-11
1 Therefore being justified by faith, we have peace with God through our Lord Jesus Christ:
2 By whom also we have access by faith into this grace wherein we stand, and rejoice in hope of the glory of God.
3 And not only so, but we glory in tribulations also: knowing that tribulation worketh patience;
4 And patience, experience; and experience, hope:
5 And hope maketh not ashamed; because the love of God is shed abroad in our hearts by the Holy Ghost which is given unto us.
6 For when we were yet without strength, in due time Christ died for the ungodly.
7 For scarcely for a righteous man will one die: yet peradventure for a

good man some would even dare to die.
8 But God commendeth his love toward us, in that, while we were yet sinners, Christ died for us.
9 Much more then, being now justified by his blood, we shall be saved from wrath through him.
10 For if, when we were enemies, we were reconciled to God by the death of his Son, much more, being reconciled, we shall be saved by his life.
11 And not only so, but we also joy in God through our Lord Jesus Christ, by whom we have now received the atonement.

How God put us right with him.
Romans 3:21-26
21 But now the righteousness of God without the law is manifested, being witnessed by the law and the prophets;
22 Even the righteousness of God which is by faith of Jesus Christ unto all and upon all them that believe: for there is no difference:
23 For all have sinned, and come short of the glory of God;
24 Being justified freely by his grace through the redemption that is in Christ Jesus:
25 Whom God hath set forth to be a propitiation through faith in his blood, to declare his righteousness for the remission of sins that are past, through the forbearance of God;
26 To declare, I say, at this time his righteousness: that he might be just, and the justifier of him which believeth in Jesus.

Hebrews 10:1-18
1 For the law having a shadow of good things to come, and not the very image of the things, can never with those sacrifices which they offered year by year continually make the comers thereunto perfect.
2 For then would they not have ceased to be offered? because that the worshippers once purged should have had no more conscience of sins.
3 But in those sacrifices there is a remembrance again made of sins every year.
4 For it is not possible that the blood of bulls and of goats should take

away sins.

5 Wherefore when he cometh into the world, he saith, Sacrifice and offering thou wouldest not, but a body hast thou prepared me:

6 In burnt offerings and sacrifices for sin thou hast had no pleasure.

7 Then said I, Lo, I come (in the volume of the book it is written of me,) to do thy will, O God.

8 Above when he said, Sacrifice and offering and burnt offerings and offering for sin thou wouldest not, neither hadst pleasure therein; which are offered by the law;

9 Then said he, Lo, I come to do thy will, O God. He taketh away the first, that he may establish the second.

10 By the which will we are sanctified through the offering of the body of Jesus Christ once for all.

11 And every priest standeth daily ministering and offering oftentimes the same sacrifices, which can never take away sins:

12 But this man, after he had offered one sacrifice for sins for ever, sat down on the right hand of God;

13 From henceforth expecting till his enemies be made his footstool.

14 For by one offering he hath perfected for ever them that are sanctified.

15 Whereof the Holy Ghost also is a witness to us: for after that he had said before,

16 This is the covenant that I will make with them after those days, saith the Lord, I will put my laws into their hearts, and in their minds will I write them;

17 And their sins and iniquities will I remember no more.

18 Now where remission of these is, there is no more offering for sin.

Hebrews 13:20-21

20 Now the God of peace, that brought again from the dead our Lord Jesus, that great shepherd of the sheep, through the blood of the everlasting covenant,

21 Make you perfect in every good work to do his will, working in you that which is wellpleasing in his sight, through Jesus Christ; to whom be glory for ever and ever. Amen.

Part 2
Lord, Lord
Matthew 7:13-14
13 Enter ye in at the strait gate: for wide is the gate, and broad is the way, that leadeth to destruction, and many there be which go in threat:
14 Because strait is the gate, and narrow is the way, which leadeth unto life, and few there be that find it.

Matthew 7:21-23
21 Not every one that saith unto me, Lord, Lord, shall enter into the kingdom of heaven; but he that doeth the will of my Father which is in heaven.
22 Many will say to me in that day, Lord, Lord, have we not prophesied in thy name? and in thy name have cast out devils? and in thy name done many wonderful works?
23 And then will I profess unto them, I never knew you: depart from me, ye that work iniquity.

Question: what is the will of the Father (God), Which Jesus is talking about in "(Matthew 7:21).

Answer: The will of the Father (God), Is the same as Jesus will, Jesus tells us what the will of the Father (God) is in the Parables he tells us and also the other things he teaches and tells us, and also what Jesus disciples teaches us.

Question: Why did Jesus say in (Matthew 7:21) Not every one that saith unto me, Lord, Lord, shall enter into the kingdom of heaven;

Answer: The answer is found in (Matthew 7:23) Jesus is speaking to the people that work iniquity.

Question: What is Iniquity.

Answer: The definition for the word iniquity is: 1 shameful Injustice: wickedness 2 an unjust or wicked act or thing.

Be wise, listen to Jesus.

Luke 6:46-49

46 And why call ye me, Lord, Lord, and do not the things which I say?
47 Whosoever cometh to me, and heareth my sayings, and doeth them, I will shew you to whom he is like:
48 He is like a man which built an house, and digged deep, and laid the foundation on a rock: and when the flood arose, the stream beat vehemently upon that house, and could not shake it: for it was founded upon a rock.
49 But he that heareth, and doeth not, is like a man that without a foundation built an house upon the earth; against which the stream did beat vehemently, and immediately it fell; and the ruin of that house was great.

St John 14:23-24

23 Jesus answered and said unto him, If a man love me, he will keep my words: and my Father will love him, and we will come unto him, and make our abode with him.
24 He that loveth me not keepeth not my sayings: and the word which ye hear is not mine, but the Father's which sent me.

Part 3

Courage before God
1 John 3:19-24
19 And hereby we know that we are of the truth, and shall assure our hearts before him.
20 For if our heart condemn us, God is greater than our heart, and knoweth all things.
21 Beloved, if our heart condemn us not, then have we confidence toward God.

22 And whatsoever we ask, we receive of him, because we keep his commandments, and do those things that are pleasing in his sight.
23 And this is his commandment, That we should believe on the name of his Son Jesus Christ, and love one another, as he gave us commandment.
24 And he that keepeth his commandments dwelleth in him, and he in him. And hereby we know that he abideth in us, by the Spirit which he hath given us.

Come to Jesus if you have not, For now is the acceptable time.
John 3:16-18
16 For God so loved the world, that he gave his only begotten Son, that whosoever believeth in him should not perish, but have everlasting life.
17 For God sent not his Son into the world to condemn the world; but that the world through him might be saved.
18 He that believeth on him is not condemned: but he that believeth not is condemned already, because he hath not believed in the name of the only begotten Son of God.

Believe in Jesus while you still can, While you still have a chance to, Jesus the Son of God is comming back again.

Romans 10:9-10
9 That if thou shalt confess with thy mouth the Lord Jesus, and shalt believe in thine heart that God hath raised him from the dead, thou shalt be saved.

So confess that Jesus is Lord and believe that God has raised him up from the dead, and you will be saved.

10 For with the heart man believeth unto righteousness; and with the mouth confession is made unto salvation.

Repent of your sins, Come to Jesus the Son of God, while you still have a chance.

Matthew 13:41-42
41 The Son of man shall send forth his angels, and they shall gather out of his kingdom all things that offend, and them which do iniquity;
42 And shall cast them into a furnace of fire: there shall be wailing and gnashing of teeth.
You don't have to be condemned to burn forever in the lake of fire and brimstone, Believe in Jesus the Son of God and turn from your wicked ways.

If you have not acceptted Jesus the Son of God the one that died for your sins. now is the time, don't let it be to late, believe in Jesus before it's to late.

If you have not been baptized in the name of the Father the Son and the Holy Ghost, Please go get baptized.

Fortify your position in Jesus the Christ.
the definition of the word fortify is -----To make strong: To strengthen and secure by military defences.

Realize that Jesus loves you.
John 3:16
16 For God so loved the world, that he gave his only begotten Son, that whosoever believeth in him should not perish, but have everlasting life.

Jesus loved you so much that he died for your sins, so you would not have to burn forever in that lake of fire and brimstone.

Now is the time of salvation, Don't let it be to late, Believe on Jesus while you still can.

Keep on doing good worksRomans 2:6-11
6 Who will render to every man according to his deeds:
7 To them who by patient continuance in well doing seek for glory and

honour and immortality, eternal life:

8 But unto them that are contentious, and do not obey the truth, but obey unrighteousness, indignation and wrath,

9 Tribulation and anguish, upon every soul of man that doeth evil, of the Jew first, and also of the Gentile;

10 But glory, honour, and peace, to every man that worketh good, to the Jew first, and also to the Gentile:

11 For there is no respect of persons with God.

In the parable the sheeps and the goats, Jesus is showing how we should help one another.

By helping one another we show that we love God, Jesus, The Holy Ghost and our fellowmen, We also show that we are saved and that our faith is alive.

The sheep and the goats. * Jesus remembering your good deeds.
Matthew 25:31-46

31 When the Son of man shall come in his glory, and all the holy angels with him, then shall he sit upon the throne of his glory:

32 And before him shall be gathered all nations: and he shall separate them one from another, as a shepherd divideth his sheep from the goats:

33 And he shall set the sheep on his right hand, but the goats on the left.

34 Then shall the King say unto them on his right hand, Come, ye blessed of my Father, inherit the kingdom prepared for you from the foundation of the world:

35 For I was an hungred, and ye gave me meat: I was thirsty, and ye gave me drink: I was a stranger, and ye took me in:

36 Naked, and ye clothed me: I was sick, and ye visited me: I was in prison, and ye came unto me.

37 Then shall the righteous answer him, saying, Lord, when saw we thee an hungred, and fed thee? or thirsty, and gave thee drink?

38 When saw we thee a stranger, and took thee in? or naked, and clothed thee?

39 Or when saw we thee sick, or in prison, and came unto thee?

40 And the King shall answer and say unto them, Verily I say unto you, Inasmuch as ye have done it unto one of the least of these my brethren, ye have done it unto me.

41 Then shall he say also unto them on the left hand, Depart from me, ye cursed, into everlasting fire, prepared for the devil and his angels:

42 For I was an hungred, and ye gave me no meat: I was thirsty, and ye gave me no drink:

43 I was a stranger, and ye took me not in: naked, and ye clothed me not: sick, and in prison, and ye visited me not.

44 Then shall they also answer him, saying, Lord, when saw we thee an hungred, or athirst, or a stranger, or naked, or sick, or in prison, and did not minister unto thee?

45 Then shall he answer them, saying, Verily I say unto you, Inasmuch as ye did it not to one of the least of these, ye did it not to me.

46 And these shall go away into everlasting punishment: but the righteous into life eternal.

Alms Giving.

Matthew 6:1-4

1 Take heed that ye do not your alms before men, to be seen of them: otherwise ye have no reward of your Father which is in heaven.

2 Therefore when thou doest thine alms, do not sound a trumpet before thee, as the hypocrites do in the synagogues and in the streets, that they may have glory of men. Verily I say unto you, They have their reward.

3 But when thou

4 That thine alms may be in secret: and thy Father which seeth in secret himself shall reward thee openly.

Luke 6:38

38 Give, and it shall be given unto you; good measure, pressed down, and shaken together, and running over, shall men give into your bosom. For with the same measure that ye mete withal it shall be measured to you again.

Love in deed and in truth. 1 John 3:17-18

17 But whoso hath this world's good, and seeth his brother have need, and shutteth up his bowels of compassion from him, how dwelleth the love of God in him?

18 My little children, let us not love in word, neither in tongue; but in deed and in truth.

James 1:22

22 But be ye doers of the word, and not hearers only, deceiving your own selves.

James 2:14-17

14 What doth it profit, my brethren, though a man say he hath faith, and have not works? can faith save him?

15 If a brother or sister be naked, and destitute of daily food,

16 And one of you say unto them, Depart in peace, be ye warmed and filled; notwithstanding ye give them not those things which are needful to the body; what doth it profit?

17 Even so faith, if it hath not works, is dead, being alone.

As James said faith without works is dead, (James 2:17) James is refering to the work of the Holy Ghost and Jesus in his parable the sheeps and the Goats (Matthew 25:31-46) Illustrated the people who's faith is alive (Matthew 25:31-40) and the people who's faith is dead (Matthew 25:41-46).

The Parable of the good samaritanIn the parable Jesus tells about the good samaritan, Jesus is further illustrating the people who's faith is alive.

Luke 10:25-37

25 And, behold, a certain lawyer stood up, and tempted him, saying, Master, what shall I do to inherit eternal life?

26 He said unto him, What is written in the law? how readest thou?

27 And he answering said, Thou shalt love the Lord thy God with all thy

heart, and with all thy soul, and with all thy strength, and with all thy mind; and thy neighbour as thyself.

28 And he said unto him, Thou hast answered right: this do, and thou shalt live.

29 But he, willing to justify himself, said unto Jesus, And who is my neighbour?

30 And Jesus answering said, A certain man went down from Jerusalem to Jericho, and fell among thieves, which stripped him of his raiment, and wounded him, and departed, leaving him half dead.

31 And by chance there came down a certain priest that way: and when he saw him, he passed by on the other side.

32 And likewise a Levite, when he was at the place, came and looked on him, and passed by on the other side.

33 But a certain Samaritan, as he journeyed, came where he was: and when he saw him, he had compassion on him,

34 And went to him, and bound up his wounds, pouring in oil and wine, and set him on his own beast, and brought him to an inn, and took care of him.

35 And on the morrow when he departed, he took out two pence, and gave them to the host, and said unto him, Take care of him; and whatsoever thou spendest more, when I come again, I will repay thee.

36 Which now of these three, thinkest thou, was neighbour unto him that fell among the thieves?

37 And he said, He that shewed mercy on him. Then said Jesus unto him, Go, and do thou likewise.

Fulfilling the lawGod gave the israelites the law which is written in the old testament, The laws are written in the books of Exodus, Leviticus, Numbers, Gods laws consist of rules and regulations that the isaelites had to live by, When they did what was written in the law, They was doing what the law required of them to do, they did the works of the law.

How we all come under gods laws.Romans 2:11-16
11 For there is no respect of persons with God.

12 For as many as have sinned without law shall also perish without law: and as many as have sinned in the law shall be judged by the law;
13 (For not the hearers of the law are just before God, but the doers of the law shall be justified.
14 For when the Gentiles, which have not the law, do by nature the things contained in the law, these, having not the law, are a law unto themselves:
15 Which shew the work of the law written in their hearts, their conscience also bearing witness, and their thoughts the mean while accusing or else excusing one another;)
16 In the day when God shall judge the secrets of men by Jesus Christ according to my gospel.

Romans 3:19
19 Now we know that what things soever the law saith, it saith to them who are under the law: that every mouth may be stopped, and all the world may become guilty before God.

Matthew 22:36-40
36 Master, which is the great commandment in the law?
37 Jesus said unto him, Thou shalt love the Lord thy God with all thy heart, and with all thy soul, and with all thy mind.
38 This is the first and great commandment.
39 And the second is like unto it, Thou shalt love thy neighbour as thyself.
40 On these two commandments hang all the law and the prophets.

If you love the lord your God with all your heart and with all your soul, and with all your mind and if you love your neighbor as yourself you will not want to do anything against God, and also you will not want to do anything against your neighbor, This is how we fulfill the law.

That is why Jesus said in (Matthew 22:40) On these two commandments hang all the law and the prophets.

And also in (Galations 5:14) further confirms Jesus statement.

Galatians 5:14
14 For all the law is fulfilled in one word, even in this; Thou shalt love thy neighbour as thyself.

Romans 10:8-13
8 But what saith it? The word is nigh thee, even in thy mouth, and in thy heart: that is, the word of faith, which we preach;
9 That if thou shalt confess with thy mouth the Lord Jesus, and shalt believe in thine heart that God hath raised him from the dead, thou shalt be saved.
10 For with the heart man believeth unto righteousness; and with the mouth confession is made unto salvation.
11 For the scripture saith, Whosoever believeth on him shall not be ashamed.
12 For there is no difference between the Jew and the Greek: for the same Lord over all is rich unto all that call upon him.
13 For whosoever shall call upon the name of the Lord shall be saved.

The way we fulfill the law is by doing what jesus said in (Matthew 22:36-40) and also what paul (saul) says in the book of Romans 13:9-10

Romans 13:9-10
9 For this, Thou shalt not commit adultery, Thou shalt not kill, Thou shalt not steal, Thou shalt not bear false witness, Thou shalt not covet; and if there be any other commandment, it is briefly comprehended in this saying, namely, Thou shalt love thy neighbour as thyself.
10 Love worketh no ill to his neighbour: therefore love is the fulfilling of the law.

How God put us right with him.
Romans 3:21-31
21 But now the righteousness of God without the law is manifested, being witnessed by the law and the prophets;
22 Even the righteousness of God which is by faith of Jesus Christ unto all

and upon all them that believe: for there is no difference:

23 For all have sinned, and come short of the glory of God;

24 Being justified freely by his grace through the redemption that is in Christ Jesus:

25 Whom God hath set forth to be a propitiation through faith in his blood, to declare his righteousness for the remission of sins that are past, through the forbearance of God;

26 To declare, I say, at this time his righteousness: that he might be just, and the justifier of him which believeth in Jesus.

27 Where is boasting then? It is excluded. By what law? of works? Nay: but by the law of faith.

28 Therefore we conclude that a man is justified by faith without the deeds of the law.

29 Is he the God of the Jews only? is he not also of the Gentiles? Yes, of the Gentiles also:

30 Seeing it is one God, which shall justify the circumcision by faith, and uncircumcision through faith.

31 Do we then make void the law through faith? God forbid: yea, we establish the law.

Galatians 2:16

16 Knowing that a man is not justified by the works of the law, but by the faith of Jesus Christ, even we have believed in Jesus Christ, that we might be justified by the faith of Christ, and not by the works of the law: for by the works of the law shall no flesh be justified.

Being led by God's spirit.

Romans 8:1-17

1 There is therefore now no condemnation to them which are in Christ Jesus, who walk not after the flesh, but after the Spirit.

2 For the law of the Spirit of life in Christ Jesus hath made me free from the law of sin and death.

3 For what the law could not do, in that it was weak through the flesh, God sending his own Son in the likeness of sinful flesh, and for sin, condemned

sin in the flesh:

4 That the righteousness of the law might be fulfilled in us, who walk not after the flesh, but after the Spirit.

5 For they that are after the flesh do mind the things of the flesh; but they that are after the Spirit the things of the Spirit.

6 For to be carnally minded is death; but to be spiritually minded is life and peace.

7 Because the carnal mind is enmity against God: for it is not subject to the law of God, neither indeed can be.

8 So then they that are in the flesh cannot please God.

9 But ye are not in the flesh, but in the Spirit, if so be that the Spirit of God dwell in you. Now if any man have not the Spirit of Christ, he is none of his.

10 And if Christ be in you, the body is dead because of sin; but the Spirit is life because of righteousness.

11 But if the Spirit of him that raised up Jesus from the dead dwell in you, he that raised up Christ from the dead shall also quicken your mortal bodies by his Spirit that dwelleth in you.

12 Therefore, brethren, we are debtors, not to the flesh, to live after the flesh.

13 For if ye live after the flesh, ye shall die: but if ye through the Spirit do mortify the deeds of the body, ye shall live.

14 For as many as are led by the Spirit of God, they are the sons of God.

15 For ye have not received the spirit of bondage again to fear; but ye have received the Spirit of adoption, whereby we cry, Abba, Father.

16 The Spirit itself beareth witness with our spirit, that we are the children of God:

17 And if children, then heirs; heirs of God, and joint-heirs with Christ; if so be that we suffer with him, that we may be also glorified together.

The fruit of the spirit and the works of the flesh.
Galatians 5:16-26

16 This I say then, Walk in the Spirit, and ye shall not fulfil the lust of the flesh.

17 For the flesh lusteth against the Spirit, and the Spirit against the flesh: and these are contrary the one to the other: so that ye cannot do the things that ye would.
18 But if ye be led of the Spirit, ye are not under the law.
19 Now the works of the flesh are manifest, which are these; Adultery, fornication, uncleanness, lasciviousness,
20 Idolatry, witchcraft, hatred, variance, emulations, wrath, strife, seditions, heresies,
21 Envyings, murders, drunkenness, revellings, and such like: of the which I tell you before, as I have also told you in time past, that they which do such things shall not inherit the kingdom of God.
22 But the fruit of the Spirit is love, joy, peace, longsuffering, gentleness, goodness, faith,
23 Meekness, temperance: against such there is no law.
24 And they that are Christ's have crucified the flesh with the affections and lusts.
25 If we live in the Spirit, let us also walk in the Spirit.
26 Let us not be desirous of vain glory, provoking one another, envying one another.

Galatians 6:21
21 Brethren, if a man be overtaken in a fault, ye which are spiritual, restore such an one in the spirit of meekness; considering thyself, lest thou also be tempted.2 Bear ye one another's burdens, and so fulfil the law of Christ.

The gifts of the Holy Ghost.
1 Corinthians 12:1-11
1 Now concerning spiritual gifts, brethren, I would not have you ignorant.
2 Ye know that ye were Gentiles, carried away unto these dumb idols, even as ye were led.
3 Wherefore I give you to understand, that no man speaking by the Spirit of God calleth Jesus accursed: and that no man can say that Jesus is the Lord, but by the Holy Ghost.
4 Now there are diversities of gifts, but the same Spirit.

5 And there are differences of administrations, but the same Lord.
6 And there are diversities of operations, but it is the same God which worketh all in all.
7 But the manifestation of the Spirit is given to every man to profit withal.
8 For to one is given by the Spirit the word of wisdom; to another the word of knowledge by the same Spirit;
9 To another faith by the same Spirit; to another the gifts of healing by the same Spirit;
10 To another the working of miracles; to another prophecy; to another discerning of spirits; to another divers kinds of tongues; to another the interpretation of tongues:
11 But all these worketh that one and the selfsame Spirit, dividing to every man severally as he will.

The unity of the body.
Ephesians 4:2-16
2 With all lowliness and meekness, with longsuffering, forbearing one another in love;
3 Endeavouring to keep the unity of the Spirit in the bond of peace.
4 There is one body, and one Spirit, even as ye are called in one hope of your calling;
5 One Lord, one faith, one baptism,
6 One God and Father of all, who is above all, and through all, and in you all.
7 But unto every one of us is given grace according to the measure of the gift of Christ.
8 Wherefore he saith, When he ascended up on high, he led captivity captive, and gave gifts unto men.
9 (Now that he ascended, what is it but that he also descended first into the lower parts of the earth?
10 He that descended is the same also that ascended up far above all heavens, that he might fill all things.)
11 And he gave some, apostles; and some, prophets; and some, evangelists; and some, pastors and teachers;

12 For the perfecting of the saints, for the work of the ministry, for the edifying of the body of Christ:

13 Till we all come in the unity of the faith, and of the knowledge of the Son of God, unto a perfect man, unto the measure of the stature of the fulness of Christ:

14 That we henceforth be no more children, tossed to and fro, and carried about with every wind of doctrine, by the sleight of men, and cunning craftiness, whereby they lie in wait to deceive;

15 But speaking the truth in love, may grow up into him in all things, which is the head, even Christ:

16 From whom the whole body fitly joined together and compacted by that which every joint supplieth, according to the effectual working in the measure of every part, maketh increase of the body unto the edifying of itself in love.

Get baptized in the name of The Father, The Son and The Holy Ghost, if you have not.

Matthew 28:16-20

16 Then the eleven disciples went away into Galilee, into a mountain where Jesus had appointed them.

17 And when they saw him, they worshipped him: but some doubted.

18 And Jesus came and spake unto them, saying, All power is given unto me in heaven and in earth.

19 Go ye therefore, and teach all nations, baptizing them in the name of the Father, and of the Son, and of the Holy Ghost:

20 Teaching them to observe all things whatsoever I have commanded you: and, lo, I am with you always, even unto the end of the world. Amen.

Dead to sin but alive in Jesus the Christ.

Romans 6:1-14

1 What shall we say then? Shall we continue in sin, that grace may abound?

2 God forbid. How shall we, that are dead to sin, live any longer therein?

3 Know ye not, that so many of us as were baptized into Jesus Christ were

baptized into his death?

4 Therefore we are buried with him by baptism into death: that like as Christ was raised up from the dead by the glory of the Father, even so we also should walk in newness of life.

5 For if we have been planted together in the likeness of his death, we shall be also in the likeness of his resurrection:

6 Knowing this, that our old man is crucified with him, that the body of sin might be destroyed, that henceforth we should not serve sin.

7 For he that is dead is freed from sin.

8 Now if we be dead with Christ, we believe that we shall also live with him:

9 Knowing that Christ being raised from the dead dieth no more; death hath no more dominion over him.

10 For in that he died, he died unto sin once: but in that he liveth, he liveth unto God.

11 Likewise reckon ye also yourselves to be dead indeed unto sin, but alive unto God through Jesus Christ our Lord.

12 Let not sin therefore reign in your mortal body, that ye should obey it in the lusts thereof.

13 Neither yield ye your members as instruments of unrighteousness unto sin: but yield yourselves unto God, as those that are alive from the dead, and your members as instruments of righteousness unto God.

14 For sin shall not have dominion over you: for ye are not under the law, but under grace.

Servants of righteousness.
Romans 6:15-23

15 What then? shall we sin, because we are not under the law, but under grace? God forbid.

16 Know ye not, that to whom ye yield yourselves servants to obey, his servants ye are to whom ye obey; whether of sin unto death, or of obedience unto righteousness?

17 But God be thanked, that ye were the servants of sin, but ye have obeyed from the heart that form of doctrine which was delivered you.

18 Being then made free from sin, ye became the servants of righteousness.
19 I speak after the manner of men because of the infirmity of your flesh: for as ye have yielded your members servants to uncleanness and to iniquity unto iniquity; even so now yield your members servants to righteousness unto holiness.
20 For when ye were the servants of sin, ye were free from righteousness.
21 What fruit had ye then in those things whereof ye are now ashamed? for the end of those things is death.
22 But now being made free from sin, and become servants to God, ye have your fruit unto holiness, and the end everlasting life.
23 For the wages of sin is death; but the gift of God is eternal life through Jesus Christ our Lord.

The whole armour of God.
Ephesians 6:10-18
10 Finally, my brethren, be strong in the Lord, and in the power of his might.
11 Put on the whole armour of God, that ye may be able to stand against the wiles of the devil.
12 For we wrestle not against flesh and blood, but against principalities, against powers, against the rulers of the darkness of this world, against spiritual wickedness in high places.
13 Wherefore take unto you the whole armour of God, that ye may be able to withstand in the evil day, and having done all, to stand.
14 Stand therefore, having your loins girt about with truth, and having on the breastplate of righteousness;
15 And your feet shod with the preparation of the gospel of peace;
16 Above all, taking the shield of faith, wherewith ye shall be able to quench all the fiery darts of the wicked.
17 And take the helmet of salvation, and the sword of the Spirit, which is the word of God:
18 Praying always with all prayer and supplication in the Spirit, and watching thereunto with all perseverance and supplication for all saints;

1 Peter 5:8

8 Be sober, be vigilant; because your adversary the devil, as a roaring lion, walketh about, seeking whom he may devour:

Judging others The definition of the word Judge: To form an authoritative opinion.

Matthew 7:1-5

1 Judge not, that ye be not judged.

2 For with what judgment ye judge, ye shall be judged: and with what measure ye mete, it shall be measured to you again.

3 And why beholdest thou the mote that is in thy brother's eye, but considerest not the beam that is in thine own eye?

4 Or how wilt thou say to thy brother, Let me pull out the mote out of thine eye; and, behold, a beam is in thine own eye?

5 Thou hypocrite, first cast out the beam out of thine own eye; and then shalt thou see clearly to cast out the mote out of thy brother's eye.

Looking unto Jesus.

Hebrews 12:1-2

1 Wherefore seeing we also are compassed about with so great a cloud of witnesses, let us lay aside every weight, and the sin which doth so easily beset us, and let us run with patience the race that is set before us,

2 Looking unto Jesus the author and finisher of our faith; who for the joy that was set before him endured the cross, despising the shame, and is set down at the right hand of the throne of God.

Children of God.

1 John 3:1-10

1 Behold, what manner of love the Father hath bestowed upon us, that we should be called the sons of God: therefore the world knoweth us not, because it knew him not.

2 Beloved, now are we the sons of God, and it doth not yet appear what we shall be: but we know that, when he shall appear, we shall be like him; for

we shall see him as he is.

3 And every man that hath this hope in him purifieth himself, even as he is pure.

4 Whosoever committeth sin transgresseth also the law: for sin is the transgression of the law.

5 And ye know that he was manifested to take away our sins; and in him is no sin.

6 Whosoever abideth in him sinneth not: whosoever sinneth hath not seen him, neither known him.

7 Little children, let no man deceive you: he that doeth righteousness is righteous, even as he is righteous.

8 He that committeth sin is of the devil; for the devil sinneth from the beginning. For this purpose the Son of God was manifested, that he might destroy the works of the devil.

9 Whosoever is born of God doth not commit sin; for his seed remaineth in him: and he cannot sin, because he is born of God.

10 In this the children of God are manifest, and the children of the devil: whosoever doeth not righteousness is not of God, neither he that loveth not his brother.

Forgive.Matthew 6:14-15

14 For if ye forgive men their trespasses, your heavenly Father will also forgive you:

15 But if ye forgive not men their trespasses, neither will your Father forgive your trespasses.

1 John 1:8-10

8 If we say that we have no sin, we deceive ourselves, and the truth is not in us.

9 If we confess our sins, he is faithful and just to forgive us our sins, and to cleanse us from all unrighteousness.

10 If we say that we have not sinned, we make him a liar, and his word is not in us.

1 John 2:1-2

1 My little children, these things write I unto you, that ye sin not. And if any man sin, we have an advocate with the Father, Jesus Christ the righteous:

2 And he is the propitiation for our sins: and not for ours only, but also for the sins of the whole world.

In union with God.

1 John 2:3-6

3 And hereby we do know that we know him, if we keep his commandments.

4 He that saith, I know him, and keepeth not his commandments, is a liar, and the truth is not in him.

5 But whoso keepeth his word, in him verily is the love of God perfected: hereby know we that we are in him.

6 He that saith he abideth in him ought himself also so to walk, even as he walked.

Beware of false prophets.

Matthew 7:15-20

15 Beware of false prophets, which come to you in sheep's clothing, but inwardly they are ravening wolves.

16 Ye shall know them by their fruits. Do men gather grapes of thorns, or figs of thistles?

17 Even so every good tree bringeth forth good fruit; but a corrupt tree bringeth forth evil fruit.

18 A good tree cannot bring forth evil fruit, neither can a corrupt tree bring forth good fruit.

19 Every tree that bringeth not forth good fruit is hewn down, and cast into the fire.

20 Wherefore by their fruits ye shall know them.

Endure unto the end.

Luke 21:7-19

7 And they asked him, saying, Master, but when shall these things be? and what sign will there be when these things shall come to pass?
8 And he said, Take heed that ye be not deceived: for many shall come in my name, saying, I am Christ; and the time draweth near: go ye not therefore after them.
9 But when ye shall hear of wars and commotions, be not terrified: for these things must first come to pass; but the end is not by and by.
10 Then said he unto them, Nation shall rise against nation, and kingdom against kingdom:
11 And great earthquakes shall be in divers places, and famines, and pestilences; and fearful sights and great signs shall there be from heaven.
12 But before all these, they shall lay their hands on you, and persecute you, delivering you up to the synagogues, and into prisons, being brought before kings and rulers for my name's sake.
13 And it shall turn to you for a testimony.
14 Settle it therefore in your hearts, not to meditate before what ye shall answer:
15 For I will give you a mouth and wisdom, which all your adversaries shall not be able to gainsay nor resist.
16 And ye shall be betrayed both by parents, and brethren, and kinsfolks, and friends; and some of you shall they cause to be put to death.
17 And ye shall be hated of all men for my name's sake.
18 But there shall not an hair of your head perish.
19 In your patience possess ye your souls.

Mark 13:13
13 And ye shall be hated of all men for my name's sake: but he that shall endure unto the end, the same shall be saved.

Stay with Jesus the Christ, Endure unto the end and be saved.

Part 4

Running toward the goal.

Philippians 3:12-21

12 Not as though I had already attained, either were already perfect: but I follow after, if that I may apprehend that for which also I am apprehended of Christ Jesus.
13 Brethren, I count not myself to have apprehended: but this one thing I do, forgetting those things which are behind, and reaching forth unto those things which are before,
14 I press toward the mark for the prize of the high calling of God in Christ Jesus.
15 Let us therefore, as many as be perfect, be thus minded: and if in any thing ye be otherwise minded, God shall reveal even this unto you.
16 Nevertheless, whereto we have already attained, let us walk by the same rule, let us mind the same thing.
17 Brethren, be followers together of me, and mark them which walk so as ye have us for an ensample.
18 (For many walk, of whom I have told you often, and now tell you even weeping, that they are the enemies of the cross of Christ:
19 Whose end is destruction, whose God is their belly, and whose glory is in their shame, who mind earthly things.)
20 For our conversation is in heaven; from whence also we look for the Saviour, the Lord Jesus Christ:
21 Who shall change our vile body, that it may be fashioned like unto his glorious body, according to the working whereby he is able even to subdue all things unto himself.

Gods love in Jesus the Christ.
Romans 8:31-39

31 What shall we then say to these things? If God be for us, who can be against us?
32 He that spared not his own Son, but delivered him up for us all, how shall he not with him also freely give us all things?
33 Who shall lay any thing to the charge of God's elect? It is God that justifieth.
34 Who is he that condemneth? It is Christ that died, yea rather, that is

risen again, who is even at the right hand of God, who also maketh intercession for us.

35 Who shall separate us from the love of Christ? shall tribulation, or distress, or persecution, or famine, or nakedness, or peril, or sword?

36 As it is written, For thy sake we are killed all the day long; we are accounted as sheep for the slaughter.

37 Nay, in all these things we are more than conquerors through him that loved us.

38 For I am persuaded, that neither death, nor life, nor angels, nor principalities, nor powers, nor things present, nor things to come,

39 Nor height, nor depth, nor any other creature, shall be able to separate us from the love of God, which is in Christ Jesus our Lord.

Salvation, Quality of work.

1 Corinthians 3:9-15

9 For we are labourers together with God: ye are God's husbandry, ye are God's building.

10 According to the grace of God which is given unto me, as a wise masterbuilder, I have laid the foundation, and another buildeth thereon. But let every man take heed how he buildeth thereupon.

11 For other foundation can no man lay than that is laid, which is Jesus Christ.

12 Now if any man build upon this foundation gold, silver, precious stones, wood, hay, stubble;

13 Every man's work shall be made manifest: for the day shall declare it, because it shall be revealed by fire; and the fire shall try every man's work of what sort it is.

14 If any man's work abide which he hath built thereupon, he shall receive a reward.

15 If any man's work shall be burned, he shall suffer loss: but he himself shall be saved; yet so as by fire.

Try not to defile the temple of God.

1 Corinthians 3:16-17

16 Know ye not that ye are the temple of God, and that the Spirit of God dwelleth in you?
17 If any man defile the temple of God, him shall God destroy; for the temple of God is holy, which temple ye are.

==========

section - 10 - Some warnings to be aware of.

==========

Some warnings to be aware of.

Please tell your children about the following warnings, It is very important that everyone knows about the warnings, Including family, friends, fellowmen.

Warnings about false Jesus Christs and prophets.
Matthew 24:5
5 For many shall come in my name, saying, I am Christ; and shall deceive many.

Matthew 24:23-27
23 Then if any man shall say unto you, Lo, here is Christ, or there; believe it not.
24 For there shall arise false Christs, and false prophets, and shall shew great signs and wonders; insomuch that, if it were possible, they shall deceive the very elect.
25 Behold, I have told you before.
26 Wherefore if they shall say unto you, Behold, he is in the desert; go not forth: behold, he is in the secret chambers; believe it not.
27 For as the lightning cometh out of the east, and shineth even unto the west; so shall also the coming of the Son of man be.

Matthew 7:15-20
15 Beware of false prophets, which come to you in sheep's clothing, but inwardly they are ravening wolves.
16 Ye shall know them by their fruits. Do men gather grapes of thorns, or

figs of thistles?

17 Even so every good tree bringeth forth good fruit; but a corrupt tree bringeth forth evil fruit.

18 A good tree cannot bring forth evil fruit, neither can a corrupt tree bring forth good fruit.

19 Every tree that bringeth not forth good fruit is hewn down, and cast into the fire.

20 Wherefore by their fruits ye shall know them.

This is just some of the highlites of the book of Revelation, Please read and study the whole book of Revelation.

Tribulation for ten days.
Revelation 2:10-11

10 Fear none of those things which thou shalt suffer: behold, the devil shall cast some of you into prison, that ye may be tried; and ye shall have tribulation ten days: be thou faithful unto death, and I will give thee a crown of life.

11 He that hath an ear, let him hear what the Spirit saith unto the churches; He that overcometh shall not be hurt of the second death.

Note: The second death is to burn forever in the lake of fire and brimstone.

Scripture probably pointing to a Pre Tribulation Rapture - Resurrection.
Revelation 3:10-13

10 Because thou hast kept the word of my patience, I also will keep thee from the hour of temptation, which shall come upon all the world, to try them that dwell upon the earth.

11 Behold, I come quickly: hold that fast which thou hast, that no man take thy crown.

12 Him that overcometh will I make a pillar in the temple of my God, and he shall go no more out: and I will write upon him the name of my God, and the name of the city of my God, which is new Jerusalem, which cometh down out of heaven from my God: and I will write upon him my

new name.
13 He that hath an ear, let him hear what the Spirit saith unto the churches.

Note: You will know that the Pre-Tribulation Rapture - Resurrection is Probably not going to happen or has been missed, If the mark of the beast starts and you are still on the earth. So if you have to die by being beheaded by Gods enemies because you did not accept the mark of the beast or for not worshipping the beast, Die, Because God will raise you back to life one day to reigned with Jesus the Christ a thousand years and I do not know when but you will also receive everlasting life.

Warning concerning the beast and the mark of the beast.
Revelation 13:15-18
15 And he had power to give life unto the image of the beast, that the image of the beast should both speak, and cause that as many as would not worship the image of the beast should be killed.
16 And he causeth all, both small and great, rich and poor, free and bond, to receive a mark in their right hand, or in their foreheads:
17 And that no man might buy or sell, save he that had the mark, or the name of the beast, or the number of his name.
18 Here is wisdom. Let him that hath understanding count the number of the beast: for it is the number of a man; and his number is Six hundred threescore and six.

Another Warning.Revelation 14:9-13
9 And the third angel followed them, saying with a loud voice, If any man worship the beast and his image, and receive his mark in his forehead, or in his hand,
10 The same shall drink of the wine of the wrath of God, which is poured out without mixture into the cup of his indignation; and he shall be tormented with fire and brimstone in the presence of the holy angels, and in the presence of the Lamb:
11 And the smoke of their torment ascendeth up forever and ever: and they have no rest day nor night, who worship the beast and his image, and

whosoever receiveth the mark of his name.

12 Here is the patience of the saints: here are they that keep the commandments of God, and the faith of Jesus.

13 And I heard a voice from heaven saying unto me, Write, Blessed are the dead which die in the Lord from henceforth: Yea, saith the Spirit, that they may rest from their labours; and their works do follow them.

Those who got victory and preparing for God the Father wrath.
Revelation 15:1-8

1 And I saw another sign in heaven, great and marvellous, seven angels having the seven last plagues; for in them is filled up the wrath of God.

2 And I saw as it were a sea of glass mingled with fire: and them that had gotten the victory over the beast, and over his image, and over his mark, and over the number of his name, stand on the sea of glass, having the harps of God.

3 And they sing the song of Moses the servant of God, and the song of the Lamb, saying, Great and marvellous are thy works, Lord God Almighty; just and true are thy ways, thou King of saints.

4 Who shall not fear thee, O Lord, and glorify thy name? for thou only art holy: for all nations shall come and worship before thee; for thy judgments are made manifest.

5 And after that I looked, and, behold, the temple of the tabernacle of the testimony in heaven was opened:

6 And the seven angels came out of the temple, having the seven plagues, clothed in pure and white linen, and having their breasts girded with golden girdles.

7 And one of the four beasts gave unto the seven angels seven golden vials full of the wrath of God, who liveth for ever and ever.

8 And the temple was filled with smoke from the glory of God, and from his power; and no man was able to enter into the temple, till the seven plagues of the seven angels were fulfilled.

The pouring of the vials, What will be happening during the time of the mark of the beast.

Revelation 16:1-21

1 And I heard a great voice out of the temple saying to the seven angels, Go your ways, and pour out the vials of the wrath of God upon the earth.
2 And the first went, and poured out his vial upon the earth; and there fell a noisome and grievous sore upon the men which had the mark of the beast, and upon them which worshipped his image.
3 And the second angel poured out his vial upon the sea; and it became as the blood of a dead man: and every living soul died in the sea.
4 And the third angel poured out his vial upon the rivers and fountains of waters; and they became blood.
5 And I heard the angel of the waters say, Thou art righteous, O Lord, which art, and wast, and shalt be, because thou hast judged thus.
6 For they have shed the blood of saints and prophets, and thou hast given them blood to drink; for they are worthy.
7 And I heard another out of the altar say, Even so, Lord God Almighty, true and righteous are thy judgments.
8 And the fourth angel poured out his vial upon the sun; and power was given unto him to scorch men with fire.
9 And men were scorched with great heat, and blasphemed the name of God, which hath power over these plagues: and they repented not to give him glory.
10 And the fifth angel poured out his vial upon the seat of the beast; and his kingdom was full of darkness; and they gnawed their tongues for pain,
11 And blasphemed the God of heaven because of their pains and their sores, and repented not of their deeds.
12 And the sixth angel poured out his vial upon the great river Euphrates; and the water thereof was dried up, that the way of the kings of the east might be prepared.
13 And I saw three unclean spirits like frogs come out of the mouth of the dragon, and out of the mouth of the beast, and out of the mouth of the false prophet.
14 For they are the spirits of devils, working miracles, which go forth unto the kings of the earth and of the whole world, to gather them to the battle of that great day of God Almighty.

15 Behold, I come as a thief. Blessed is he that watcheth, and keepeth his garments, lest he walk naked, and they see his shame.

16 And he gathered them together into a place called in the Hebrew tongue Armageddon.

17 And the seventh angel poured out his vial into the air; and there came a great voice out of the temple of heaven, from the throne, saying, It is done.

18 And there were voices, and thunders, and lightnings; and there was a great earthquake, such as was not since men were upon the earth, so mighty an earthquake, and so great.

19 And the great city was divided into three parts, and the cities of the nations fell: and great Babylon came in remembrance before God, to give unto her the cup of the wine of the fierceness of his wrath.

20 And every island fled away, and the mountains were not found.

21 And there fell upon men a great hail out of heaven, every stone about the weight of a talent: and men blasphemed God because of the plague of the hail; for the plague thereof was exceeding great.

Jesus and his armies.
Revelation 19:1-21

1 And after these things I heard a great voice of much people in heaven, saying, Alleluia; Salvation, and glory, and honour, and power, unto the Lord our God:

2 For true and righteous are his judgments: for he hath judged the great whore, which did corrupt the earth with her fornication, and hath avenged the blood of his servants at her hand.

3 And again they said, Alleluia And her smoke rose up for ever and ever.

4 And the four and twenty elders and the four beasts fell down and worshipped God that sat on the throne, saying, Amen; Alleluia.

5 And a voice came out of the throne, saying, Praise our God, all ye his servants, and ye that fear him, both small and great.

6 And I heard as it were the voice of a great multitude, and as the voice of many waters, and as the voice of mighty thunderings, saying, Alleluia: for the Lord God omnipotent reigneth.

7 Let us be glad and rejoice, and give honour to him: for the marriage of

the Lamb is come, and his wife hath made herself ready.

8 And to her was granted that she should be arrayed in fine linen, clean and white: for the fine linen is the righteousness of saints.

9 And he saith unto me, Write, Blessed are they which are called unto the marriage supper of the Lamb. And he saith unto me, These are the true sayings of God.

10 And I fell at his feet to worship him. And he said unto me, See thou do it not: I am thy fellowservant, and of thy brethren that have the testimony of Jesus: worship God: for the testimony of Jesus is the spirit of prophecy.

11 And I saw heaven opened, and behold a white horse; and he that sat upon him was called Faithful and True, and in righteousness he doth judge and make war.

12 His eyes were as a flame of fire, and on his head were many crowns; and he had a name written, that no man knew, but he himself.

13 And he was clothed with a vesture dipped in blood: and his name is called The Word of God.

14 And the armies which were in heaven followed him upon white horses, clothed in fine linen, white and clean.

15 And out of his mouth goeth a sharp sword, that with it he should smite the nations: and he shall rule them with a rod of iron: and he treadeth the winepress of the fierceness and wrath of Almighty God.

16 And he hath on his vesture and on his thigh a name written, King Of Kings, And Lord Of Lords.

17 And I saw an angel standing in the sun; and he cried with a loud voice, saying to all the fowls that fly in the midst of heaven, Come and gather yourselves together unto the supper of the great God;

18 That ye may eat the flesh of kings, and the flesh of captains, and the flesh of mighty men, and the flesh of horses, and of them that sit on them, and the flesh of all men, both free and bond, both small and great.

19 And I saw the beast, and the kings of the earth, and their armies, gathered together to make war against him that sat on the horse, and against his army.

20 And the beast was taken, and with him the false prophet that wrought miracles before him, with which he deceived them that had received the

mark of the beast, and them that worshipped his image. These both were cast alive into a lake of fire burning with brimstone.
21 And the remnant were slain with the sword of him that sat upon the horse, which sword proceeded out of his mouth: and all the fowls were filled with their flesh.

Blessings for those who die by being beheaded. - The first Rapture - Resurrection.
Revelation 20:4-6
4 And I saw thrones, and they sat upon them, and judgment was given unto them: and I saw the souls of them that were beheaded for the witness of Jesus, and for the word of God, and which had not worshipped the beast, neither his image, neither had received his mark upon their foreheads, or in their hands; and they lived and reigned with Christ a thousand years.
5 But the rest of the dead lived not again until the thousand years were finished. This is the first resurrection.
6 Blessed and holy is he that hath part in the first resurrection: on such the second death hath no power, but they shall be priests of God and of Christ, and shall reign with him a thousand years.

Note: The second death has no power because they have eternal life.

Reminder: you will know that it is the mark of the beast because you will not be able to buy or sell without it, Do not get it for any reason.

Pray that everyone be warned about the mark of the beast and what it is.
The prayer.
Father God in heaven, please warn more people about the mark of the beast and what it is.   This I humbly ask in Jesus the Christ Holy name, amen.

Note: I strongly believe that one of the mark of the beast might be an RFID microchip about the size of a grain of rice or it might be smaller, If you are told by a financial institution that you need one to buy and sell or if your doctor try to give you one to keep track of medical records or to confirm that you received a vaccine or your Job, school or church try to give you one, Please don't get one for any reason.

Even if it means dying by being beheaded by God the Father enemies.

Loveing and fearing God the Father enough to die for him just as Jesus did.

Loveing God the Father.
Matthew 22:36-38
36 Master, which is the great commandment in the law?
37 Jesus said unto him, Thou shalt love the Lord thy God with all thy heart, and with all thy soul, and with all thy mind.
38 This is the first and great commandment.

Fearing God the Father.Matthew 10:28
28 And fear not them which kill the body, but are not able to kill the soul: but rather fear him which is able to destroy both soul and body in hell.

Reminder: I just touched on some of the highlites of the book of Revelation, Please read and study the whole book of Revelation.

Again, Please tell your children about the warnings, It is very important that everyone knows about the warnings, Including Family, Friends and our Fellowmen.

Look to Jesus just like I am, because there is only salvation in him.

Please read and study the Holy Bible.   Take it seriously.   May God the Father bless you.   And I hope to see you in the new heaven and the new earth to come.   Aman.

Please do not get a AI mind chip implant in your brain. It is very

dangerous to do this, such as, it might get a virus or it may be used to control you or urge you to take the mark of the beast, etc. we have been doing just fine all this time without one. when God the Father and Jesus the Christ come and visit us. It is in the brain and the Holy Spirit lives there all the time. Please leave it as natural as possible. especially if you are a Christian, I will resist to the death, before I would get one and so should everybody.

Please do not get a humanoid robot. I tell you this, for your own good. Please do not do it.

It is safer to read the Holy Bible, Do not listen to the Holy Bible on the internet, cassette tapes, mp3, etc.

Please throw away or delete your audio files, This is truly, honestly the best for you, These audio files are truly dangerous, Because it talks about good and bad forces, and they might effect you in a good way. and in a bad way. Just read it to yourself and out loud to each other.

When you read your Holy Bible, you should pray to God the Father over the Holy Bible, that you are protected by him.

If you do listen to the Holy Bible on the internet, cassette tapes, mp3, etc. Listen for short periods at a time and before you start, pray to God the Father that you are protected from bad forces, asking in Jesus the Christ name, God The Father will do this for you.

If you feel that you have sinned in a big way, I encourage you again to continue your Christian walk anyway for salvation.

One of the things the devil (Gods enemy) does is try to make you think that things are more worse than they really are, and it's just not.

If you left, for any reason, return to Jesus the Christ (The sent one) and be

healed in every way.
Living a loving life is the answer. Live your loving life.

    Pray that people return to God the Father, Jesus Christ and the Holy Spirit.

The prayer
    God the Father, Please guide the people back to you who left, this I humbly ask in Jesus Holy name. Aman

Please tell others about Jesus the Christ (The sent one).
Revelation 22:16-17
16 "I, Jesus, have sent my angel to give you[a] this testimony for the churches. I am the Root and the Offspring of David, and the bright Morning Star."
17 The Spirit and the bride say, "Come!" And let the one who hears say, "Come!" Let the one who is thirsty come; and let the one who wishes take the free gift of the water of life.
Again: Look to Jesus just like I am, because there is only salvation in him.

Repenting of sins.   Saving others is saving yourself.
James 5:19-20
19 My brothers and sisters, if one of you should wander from the truth and someone should bring that person back,
20 remember this: Whoever turns a sinner from the error of their way will save them from death and cover over a multitude of sins.

Please tell peole about this booklet.

I ask that only Christians pray for the people on the list, thank you.

About Prayer.
James 5:16
Therefore confess your sins to each other and pray for each other so that

you may be healed. The prayer of a righteous person is powerful and effective.

About petitions, prayers, intercession.
1 Timothy 2:1-3
1 I urge, then, first of all, that petitions, prayers, intercession and thanksgiving be made for all people
2 for kings and all those in authority, that we may live peaceful and quiet lives in all godliness and holiness.
3 This is good, and pleases God our Savior,

Share with your fellow men and loved ones and if you can, E-mail a copy to them.

It is about being ready for Jesus the Christ soon return.

Use this booklet to examine your self to see if you are in God the Father will, If you start doubting yourself, come back to this book to see if there is any changes you need to make to your life.

Before you get married, have your fiance read this booklet and agree to live by it.

==========

Section - 11 - Forgiveness for blasphemy of the Holy Ghost.

This added section is good news, to the Jewish people and everyone else, a lot of people would not be saved if it was not for this provision in the Holy Bible.
==========
Note: The Holy Ghost is also known as the Holy Spirit.

"Forgiveness for blasphemy of the Holy Ghost."

Blasphemy: Occurs when a person speaks against God, Jesus, Holy Ghost or another person offensively.

Is there forgiveness for the unpardonable eternal sin Jesus is speaking about in Mark 3:28-29?

What Jesus said before God and him started forgiving Blasphemy against the Holy Spirit.

Mark 3:28-29
28 Verily I say unto you, All sins shall be forgiven unto the sons of men, and blasphemies wherewith soever they shall blaspheme:
29 But he that shall blaspheme against the Holy Ghost hath never forgiveness, but is in danger of eternal damnation.

The answer is yes. Blasphemy against God, Jesus and the Holy Spirit is forgivable whether it is on purpose or not. God and Jesus wanted to save the people that blasphemed the Holy Ghost, Jesus accomplished this by calling and saving Saul (Paul).

Paul before he accepted Jesus.
Acts 26:9-11
9 "I too was convinced that I ought to do all that was possible to oppose the name of Jesus of Nazareth.
10 And that is just what I did in Jerusalem. On the authority of the chief priests I put many of the Lord's people in prison, and

when they were put to death, I cast my vote against them.
11 Many a time I went from one synagogue to another to have them punished, and I tried to force them to blaspheme. I was so obsessed with persecuting them that I even hunted them down in foreign cities.

I Timothy 1:13
13 Even though I was once a blasphemer and a persecutor and a violent man, I was shown mercy because I acted in ignorance and unbelief.

Paul being called and saved by Jesus.
Acts 9:1-18
1 And Saul, yet breathing out threatenings and slaughter against the disciples of the Lord, went unto the high priest,
2 And desired of him letters to Damascus to the synagogues, that if he found any of this way, whether they were men or women, he might bring them bound unto Jerusalem.
3 And as he journeyed, he came near Damascus: and suddenly there shined round about him a light from heaven:
4 And he fell to the earth, and heard a voice saying unto him, Saul, Saul, why persecutest thou me?
5 And he said, Who art thou, Lord? And the Lord said, I am Jesus whom thou persecutest: it is hard for thee to kick against the pricks.
6 And he trembling and astonished said, Lord, what wilt thou have me to do? And the Lord said unto him, Arise, and go into the city, and it shall be told thee what thou must do.
7 And the men which journeyed with him stood speechless, hearing a voice, but seeing no man.
8 And Saul arose from the earth; and when his eyes were opened, he saw no man: but they led him by the hand, and brought him into Damascus.
9 And he was three days without sight, and neither did eat nor

drink.

10 And there was a certain disciple at Damascus, named Ananias; and to him said the Lord in a vision, Ananias. And he said, Behold, I am here, Lord.

11 And the Lord said unto him, Arise, and go into the street which is called Straight, and enquire in the house of Judas for one called Saul, of Tarsus: for, behold, he prayeth,

12 And hath seen in a vision a man named Ananias coming in, and putting his hand on him, that he might receive his sight.

13 Then Ananias answered, Lord, I have heard by many of this man, how much evil he hath done to thy saints at Jerusalem:

14 And here he hath authority from the chief priests to bind all that call on thy name.

15 But the Lord said unto him, Go thy way: for he is a chosen vessel unto me, to bear my name before the Gentiles, and kings, and the children of Israel:

16 For I will shew him how great things he must suffer for my name's sake.

17 And Ananias went his way, and entered into the house; and putting his hands on him said, Brother Saul, the Lord, even Jesus, that appeared unto thee in the way as thou camest, hath sent me, that thou mightest receive thy sight, and be filled with the Holy Ghost.

18 And immediately there fell from his eyes as it had been scales: and he received sight forthwith, and arose, and was baptized.

Note: The reason why it was Jesus the Christ that blinded Paul and not Satan (Devil), Is because nowhere in the Holy Bible does it say satan has that ability nor does Satan shows that ability in the Holy Bible.

God the Father, Jesus the Christ and and Holy Angels on

the other hand demonstrate that they have the ability to affect people eyes, and it is all through the Holy Bible, This is how You know that it was Jesus the Christ and not Satan that talked to and blinded Paul (saul), Now he see's just fine because his sight was restored.

Forgivable sin
Concerning I Timothy 1:13, 13
13 Even though I was once a blasphemer and a persecutor and a violent man, I was shown mercy because I acted in ignorance and unbelief.

Paul was not forgiven because he persecuted Christians and blasphemed in ignorance.

Jesus mentions nothing about doing something in ignorance, Jesus forgave Paul because he wanted to and in doing so anyone who blasphemes the Holy Ghost by accident or on purpose can be forgiven and saved.

This is one of the things that was accomplished when Jesus called and saved Paul.

Another example where God the Father changed his mind.
Jonah 3:10

10 And God saw their works, that they turned from their evil way; and God repented of the evil, that he had said that he would do unto them; and he did it not.

Another example of comming back to God the Father in the parable Jesus tells.

Luke 15:1-32

1 Then drew near unto him all the publicans and sinners for to hear him.
2 And the Pharisees and scribes murmured, saying, This man receiveth sinners, and eateth with them.
3 And he spake this parable unto them, saying,
4 What man of you, having an hundred sheep, if he lose one of them, doth not leave the ninety and nine in the wilderness, and go after that which is lost, until he find it?
5 And when he hath found it, he layeth it on his shoulders, rejoicing.
6 And when he cometh home, he calleth together his friends and neighbours, saying unto them, Rejoice with me; for I have found my sheep which was lost.
7 I say unto you, that likewise joy shall be in heaven over one sinner that repenteth, more than over ninety and nine just persons, which need no repentance.
8 Either what woman having ten pieces of silver, if she lose one piece, doth not light a candle, and sweep the house, and seek diligently till she find it?
9 And when she hath found it, she calleth her friends and her neighbours together, saying, Rejoice with me; for I have found the piece which I had lost.

10 Likewise, I say unto you, there is joy in the presence of the angels of God over one sinner that repenteth.
11 And he said, A certain man had two sons:
12 And the younger of them said to his father, Father, give me the portion of goods that falleth to me. And he divided unto them his living.
13 And not many days after the younger son gathered all

together, and took his journey into a far country, and there wasted his substance with riotous living.

14 And when he had spent all, there arose a mighty famine in that land; and he began to be in want.

15 And he went and joined himself to a citizen of that country; and he sent him into his fields to feed swine.

16 And he would fain have filled his belly with the husks that the swine did eat: and no man gave unto him.

17 And when he came to himself, he said, How many hired servants of my father's have bread enough and to spare, and I perish with hunger!

18 I will arise and go to my father, and will say unto him, Father, I have sinned against heaven, and before thee,

19 And am no more worthy to be called thy son: make me as one of thy hired servants.

20 And he arose, and came to his father. But when he was yet a great way off, his father saw him, and had compassion, and ran, and fell on his neck, and kissed him.

21 And the son said unto him, Father, I have sinned against heaven, and in thy sight, and am no more worthy to be called thy son.

22 But the father said to his servants, Bring forth the best robe, and put it on him; and put a ring on his hand, and shoes on his feet:

23 And bring hither the fatted calf, and kill it; and let us eat, and be merry:

24 For this my son was dead, and is alive again; he was lost, and is found. And they began to be merry.

25 Now his elder son was in the field: and as he came and drew nigh to the house, he heard music and dancing.

26 And he called one of the servants, and asked what these things meant.

27 And he said unto him, Thy brother is come; and thy father hath killed the fatted calf, because he hath received him safe

and sound.

28 And he was angry, and would not go in: therefore came his father out, and intreated him.

29 And he answering said to his father, Lo, these many years do I serve thee, neither transgressed I at any time thy commandment: and yet thou never gavest me a kid, that I might make merry with my friends:

30 But as soon as this thy son was come, which hath devoured thy living with harlots, thou hast killed for him the fatted calf.

31 And he said unto him, Son, thou art ever with me, and all that I have is thine.

32 It was meet that we should make merry, and be glad: for this thy brother was dead, and is alive again; and was lost, and is found.

Thanks for reading, please share this information, one way is to E-mail this information to family and friends and strangers, or have a Holy bible study, etc.

If you would like a hard copy, Go to Amazon.com, Type this book tittled: Urgent, Need to know information, For Christians and non Christians.
===========
Heaven is a gift from God the Father to the saved of mankind.
Strive for it.
===========

Living a Loving Life.

The cost of living a loving life for God the Father, Jesus the Christ and the Holy Sprit.

The cost may be letting your loved ones and friends not be written in the book of life, if that is what they want, talk to them, pray for them, that they come to there senses and escape the trap that satan the devil has set.

The fact is that not everyone is going to be saved. I do not like it but that is just the way it is.

We may have to die for God the Father, Jesus the Christ and the Holy Spirit.

Jesus died for us, so we can get forgiven for our sins, we may have to die for God the Father, Jesus the Christ and the Holy Sprit, to be faithful to the death to prove our faith in them.

That may be the cost of loving them, that is just the way it is.

We are in a battle of good against evil, good must win at all cost, because God the Father, Jesus the Christ and the Holy Sprit only wants the best for mankind; satan the devil. only wants you to burn forever with him, in the lake of fire and brimstone.

God the Father destroyed everyone on earth with the great flood because of sins, except for eight people, on noah's ark, that is how serious this battle is, next time it will be by fire and brimstone.

Put God the Father, Jesus the Christ and the Holy Sprit, first in your life; you must do this to survive here on earth and hopefully later in heaven, If you make it to the new heaven and the new earth, you should be safe.

Live your life of love.

Be brave to the end to be saved and receive everlasting life.

Revelation 21:1-27
1 And I saw a new heaven and a new earth: for the first heaven and the first earth were passed away; and there was no more sea.
2 And I John saw the holy city, new Jerusalem, coming down from God out of heaven, prepared as a bride adorned for her husband.

3 And I heard a great voice out of heaven saying, Behold, the tabernacle of God is with men, and he will dwell with them, and they shall be his people, and God himself shall be with them, and be their God.

4 And God shall wipe away all tears from their eyes; and there shall be no more death, neither sorrow, nor crying, neither shall there be any more pain: for the former things are passed away.

5 And he that sat upon the throne said, Behold, I make all things new. And he said unto me, Write: for these words are true and faithful.

6 And he said unto me, It is done. I am Alpha and Omega, the beginning and the end. I will give unto him that is athirst of the fountain of the water of life freely.

7 He that overcometh shall inherit all things; and I will be his God, and he shall be my son.

8 But the fearful, and unbelieving, and the abominable, and murderers, and whoremongers, and sorcerers, and idolaters, and all liars, shall have their part in the lake which burneth with fire and brimstone: which is the second death.

9 And there came unto me one of the seven angels which had the seven vials full of the seven last plagues, and talked with me, saying, Come hither, I will shew thee the bride, the Lamb's wife.

10 And he carried me away in the spirit to a great and high mountain, and shewed me that great city, the holy Jerusalem, descending out of heaven from God,

11 Having the glory of God: and her light was like unto a stone most precious, even like a jasper stone, clear as crystal;

12 And had a wall great and high, and had twelve gates, and at the gates twelve angels, and names written thereon, which are the names of the twelve tribes of the children of Israel:

13 On the east three gates; on the north three gates; on the south three gates; and on the west three gates.

14 And the wall of the city had twelve foundations, and in them the names of the twelve apostles of the Lamb.

15 And he that talked with me had a golden reed to measure the city, and the gates thereof, and the wall thereof.

16 And the city lieth foursquare, and the length is as large as the breadth: and he measured the city with the reed, twelve thousand furlongs. The length and the breadth and the height of it are equal.

17 And he measured the wall thereof, an hundred and forty and four cubits, according to the measure of a man, that is, of the angel.

18 And the building of the wall of it was of jasper: and the city was pure gold, like unto clear glass.

19 And the foundations of the wall of the city were garnished with all manner of precious stones. The first foundation was jasper; the second, sapphire; the third, a chalcedony; the fourth, an emerald;

20 The fifth, sardonyx; the sixth, sardius; the seventh, chrysolyte; the eighth, beryl; the ninth, a topaz; the tenth, a chrysoprasus; the eleventh, a jacinth; the twelfth, an amethyst.

21 And the twelve gates were twelve pearls: every several gate was of one pearl: and the street of the city was pure gold, as it were transparent glass.

22 And I saw no temple therein: for the Lord God Almighty and the Lamb are the temple of it.

23 And the city had no need of the sun, neither of the moon, to shine in it: for the glory of God did lighten it, and the Lamb is the light thereof.

24 And the nations of them which are saved shall walk in the light of it: and the kings of the earth do bring their glory and honour into it.

25 And the gates of it shall not be shut at all by day: for there shall be no night there.

26 And they shall bring the glory and honour of the nations into it.

27 And there shall in no wise enter into it any thing that defileth, neither whatsoever worketh abomination, or maketh a lie: but they which are written in the Lamb's book of life.

Revelation 22:1-21

1 And he shewed me a pure river of water of life, clear as crystal, proceeding out of the throne of God and of the Lamb.

2 In the midst of the street of it, and on either side of the river, was there the tree of life, which bare twelve manner of fruits, and yielded her fruit every month: and the leaves of the tree were for the healing of the nations.

3 And there shall be no more curse: but the throne of God and of the Lamb shall be in it; and his servants shall serve him:

4 And they shall see his face; and his name shall be in their foreheads.

5 And there shall be no night there; and they need no candle, neither light of the sun; for the Lord God giveth them light: and they shall reign for ever and ever.

6 And he said unto me, These sayings are faithful and true: and the Lord God of the holy prophets sent his angel to shew unto his servants the things which must shortly be done.

7 Behold, I come quickly: blessed is he that keepeth the sayings of the prophecy of this book.

8 And I John saw these things, and heard them. And when I had heard and seen, I fell down to worship before the feet of the angel which shewed me these things.

9 Then saith he unto me, See thou do it not: for I am thy fellowservant, and of thy brethren the prophets, and of them which keep the sayings of this book: worship God.

10 And he saith unto me, Seal not the sayings of the prophecy of this book: for the time is at hand.

11 He that is unjust, let him be unjust still: and he which is filthy, let him be filthy still: and he that is righteous, let him be righteous still: and he that is holy, let him be holy still.

12 And, behold, I come quickly; and my reward is with me, to give every man according as his work shall be.

13 I am Alpha and Omega, the beginning and the end, the first and the last.

14 Blessed are they that do his commandments, that they may have right to the tree of life, and may enter in through the gates into the city.

15 For without are dogs, and sorcerers, and whoremongers, and murderers, and idolaters, and whosoever loveth and maketh a lie.

16 I Jesus have sent mine angel to testify unto you these things in the churches. I am the root and the offspring of David, and the bright and morning star.

17 And the Spirit and the bride say, Come. And let him that heareth say, Come. And let him that is athirst come. And whosoever will, let him take

the water of life freely.

18 For I testify unto every man that heareth the words of the prophecy of this book, If any man shall add unto these things, God shall add unto him the plagues that are written in this book:

19 And if any man shall take away from the words of the book of this prophecy, God shall take away his part out of the book of life, and out of the holy city, and from the things which are written in this book.

20 He which testifieth these things saith, Surely I come quickly. Amen. Even so, come, Lord Jesus.

21 The grace of our Lord Jesus Christ be with you all. Amen.

==========

Read and study the Holy Bible.

==========

This booklet is dedicated to God the Father, Jesus the Christ, the Holy Spirit and the saved ones, amen.

==========

I say this to my fellowmen, strive to be a saved one.

==========

Last note: Talk to God the Father, Jesus the Christ and the Holy Spirit, with respect, dignity, kindness and reverence, They are our creators, family and our friends.

==========

Pray to God the Father for the second coming of Jesus the Christ, asking him in Jesus the Christ name.

==========

Matthew 18:19-20

19 Again I say unto you, That if two of you shall agree on earth as touching any thing that they shall ask, it shall be done for them of my Father which is in heaven.

20 For where two or three are gathered together in my name, there am I in the midst of them.

==========

Romans 12:1-3

1 I beseech you therefore, brethren, by the mercies of God, that ye present your bodies a living sacrifice, holy, acceptable unto God, which is your reasonable service.

2 And be not conformed to this world: but be ye transformed by the renewing of your mind, that ye may prove what is that good, and acceptable, and perfect, will of God.

3 For I say, through the grace given unto me, to every man that is among you, not to think of himself more highly than he ought to think; but to think soberly, according as God hath dealt to every man the measure of faith.

===========

It is done.

===========

The Following is a repeat of what you just read, strive to live your life of love, may God bless you for reading.

===========

You are being saved from burning forever, please take this booklet seriously.

Jesus the Christ loves you and has called you.
John 15:19
19 If ye were of the world, the world would love his own: but because ye are not of the world, but I have chosen you out of the world, therefore the world hateth you.

Being with God the Father, Jesus the Christ and the Holy Spirit, on there terms. Please read all of this booklet, for the best life for you.

    Some of the sins (Wrong doing) that if you are doing, you need to turn away from and ask God for forgiveness in Jesus name, Idolatry - Putting anything or person in the place of God the Father the creator, abortion, lesbianism Romans 1:26, Matthew 18:6-8, homosexuality Romans 1:27, Matthew 18:6-8, adultery, masturbation, fighting and doing illegal drugs. Note: Matthew 18:6-8 applies to anyone that causes others to sin.

God the Father's ten commandment's. Exodus 20:1-17 I am the Lord your God. You shall worship no other gods beside me. You shall not carry God*s name in vain. Remember the Sabbath day to keep it holy. Honor your father and mother. You shall not murder. You shall not commit adultery. You shall not steal. You shall not bear false witness against your neighbor. You shall not covet your neighbor*s house: you shall not covet your neighbor*s wife * Or anything that is your neighbor*s.
The Good news is that Jesus the Christ died for your sins and was raised back to life by God the Father so that you can live forever with them, this booklet tells you how.

God loves mankind, Satan hates mankind, Be on Gods side.

This book is meant to give people a better understanding of the Holy Bible, hopefully it will become required reading in every church and school, It has been a work of love.

Read some and then reflect on what is said or talk about what you read in Bible study, Then read some more.

This book is not to be recorded. For reasons I will not go into, It is better for everyone this way, Again I say this book is never to be recorded, please respect my decision on this matter, This is also God the Father your creator, will.

If some one is reckless enough to record this book, Please throw the recordings away, Again: This is also God the Father your creator, will.

This book is not to be changed, because it might loss some of its meaning. This is also God the Father your creator, will.

God the Father has given me permission to change this.

I talked to God the Father and he told me to tell people that its ok to record my book, all I ask is that you please record all of it, not just some of it.

What Jesus the Christ says about peace.
John 16:33
33 These things I have spoken unto you, that in me ye might have peace. In the world ye shall have tribulation: but be of good cheer; I have overcome the world.

Having the peace of God.
Philippians 4:6-8
6 Be careful for nothing; but in every thing by prayer and supplication with thanksgiving let your requests be made known unto God.
7 And the peace of God, which passeth all understanding, shall keep your hearts and minds through Christ Jesus.
8 Finally, brethren, whatsoever things are true, whatsoever things are honest, whatsoever things are just, whatsoever things are pure, whatsoever things are lovely, whatsoever things are of good report; if there be any virtue, and if there be any praise, think on these things.

Note: No matter what happens, read this booklet, do not let the devil (satan) cheat you out of your everlasting life. Do not be condemned to burn forever with the devil.

If you left, for any reason, Even if the reason is me, return back to Jesus the Christ and be healed in every way.

Living a loving life is the answer. Live your loving life.

There is only salvation in God the Father son Jesus the Christ (The sent one).

Repenting of sins.   Saving others is saving yourself.
James 5:19-20
19 My brothers and sisters, if one of you should wander from the truth and someone should bring that person back,
20 remember this: Whoever turns a sinner from the error of their way will save them from death and cover over a multitude of sins.

Note: If you come across any of my books that do not warn you about the devil, throw them away, Thank you.

Philippians 4:8
8 Finally, brothers and sisters, whatever is true, whatever is noble, whatever is right, whatever is pure, whatever is lovely, whatever is admirable if anything is excellent or praiseworthy—think about such things.

Colossians 3:12
12 Therefore, as God's chosen people, holy and dearly loved, clothe yourselves with compassion, kindness, humility, gentleness and patience. Living a loving life is the answer. Live your loving life.

   Pray that people return to God the Father, Jesus Christ and the Holy Spirit.

The prayer.
God the Father, please guide the people back to you Jesus Christ and the Holy Spirit if they left, This I humbly ask in Jesus the Christ Holy name, Amen.

If you would like a hard copy of this booklet tittled: Urgent, Need to know information, For Christians and non Christians.   Please go to amazon.com

Philippians 4:8

8 Finally, brothers and sisters, whatever is true, whatever is noble, whatever is right, whatever is pure, whatever is lovely, whatever is admirable if anything is excellent or praiseworthy—think about such things.

==========

Section - 1 - What happens to Christians.

==========

Section - 2 - Confession of faith, get baptized.

==========

Section - 3 - In the family of God the Father.

==========

Section - 4 - Warning's about your enemy the devil, (satan).

==========

Section - 5 - Listing of sins, that if you are doing, you need to confess and turn away from, if you fail to turn away from that or those sins, try again, and if you keep failing keep trying, do not give up.

==========

Section - 6 - Love yourself enough, to not stop your christen life of love, do not give up, remember loving others is loving yourself.

==========

Section - 7 - Look to God the Father Son, Jesus the Christ, just like I am, to be saved, Because there is only salvation through him.

==========

Section - 8 - Build or continue your relation with God the Father, Jesus the Christ, The Holy Sprit and the saints.

==========

Section - 9 - Diffarent subjects to study, to help you understand the Holy Bible more.

==========

Section - 10 - Some warnings to be aware of.

==========

Section - 11 - Forgiveness for blasphemy of the Holy Ghost.
This added section is good news, to the Jewish people and everyone else, a lot of people would not be saved if it was not for this provision in the Holy Bible.

===========

Note: Before you start your study remember it is all about love, God the Father, Jesus the Christ and the Holy Spirit love for mankind, mankind kind love for each other.

God the Father love.
St John 3:16-18
16 For God so loved the world, that he gave his only begotten Son, that whosoever believeth in him should not perish, but have everlasting life.
17 For God sent not his Son into the world to condemn the world; but that the world through him might be saved.
18 He that believeth on him is not condemned: but he that believeth not is condemned already, because he hath not believed in the name of the only begotten Son of God.

    Some of the sins (Wrong doing) that if you are doing, you need to turn away from and ask God for forgiveness in Jesus name, some sins are, Idolatry - Putting anything or person in the place of God the Father the creator, murder, abortion, lesbianism Romans 1:26, homosexuality Romans 1:27, adultery, masturbation, fighting and doing illegal drugs. Note: Matthew 18:6-8 applies to anyone that causes others to sin.

Ten Commandments in order, Exodus 20:1-17
   I am the Lord your God. You shall worship no other gods beside me. You shall not carry God's name in vain. Remember the Sabbath day to keep it holy. Honor your father and mother. You shall not murder. You shall not commit adultery. You shall not steal. You shall not bear false witness against your neighbor. You shall not covet your neighbor's house: you shall not covet your neighbor's wife ... Or

anything that is your neighbor's.

God loves mankind, Satan hates mankind, Be on Gods side.

What Jesus says about fighting and revenge.
Matthew 5:38-39
38 "You have heard that it was said, 'Eye for eye, and tooth for tooth.'
39 But I tell you, do not resist an evil person. If anyone slaps you on the right cheek, turn to them the other cheek also.

Romans 12:19 Do not take revenge, my dear friends, but leave room for God's wrath, for it is written: "It is mine to avenge; I will repay," says the Lord.

Loving others is loving yourself.
Matthew 25:31-46
31 When the Son of man shall come in his glory, and all the holy angels with him, then shall he sit upon the throne of his glory:
32 And before him shall be gathered all nations: and he shall separate them one from another, as a shepherd divideth his sheep from the goats:
33 And he shall set the sheep on his right hand, but the goats on the left.
34 Then shall the King say unto them on his right hand, Come, ye blessed of my Father, inherit the kingdom prepared for you from the foundation of the world:
35 For I was an hungred, and ye gave me meat: I was thirsty, and ye gave me drink: I was a stranger, and ye took me in:
36 Naked, and ye clothed me: I was sick, and ye visited me: I was in prison, and ye came unto me.
37 Then shall the righteous answer him, saying, Lord, when saw we thee an hungred, and fed thee? or thirsty, and gave thee drink?
38 When saw we thee a stranger, and took thee in? or naked, and clothed thee?
39 Or when saw we thee sick, or in prison, and came unto thee?
40 And the King shall answer and say unto them, Verily I say unto you,

Inasmuch as ye have done it unto one of the least of these my brethren, ye have done it unto me.

41 Then shall he say also unto them on the left hand, Depart from me, ye cursed, into everlasting fire, prepared for the devil and his angels:

42 For I was an hungred, and ye gave me no meat: I was thirsty, and ye gave me no drink:

43 I was a stranger, and ye took me not in: naked, and ye clothed me not: sick, and in prison, and ye visited me not.

44 Then shall they also answer him, saying, Lord, when saw we thee an hungred, or athirst, or a stranger, or naked, or sick, or in prison, and did not minister unto thee?

45 Then shall he answer them, saying, Verily I say unto you, Inasmuch as ye did it not to one of the least of these, ye did it not to me.

46 And these shall go away into everlasting punishment: but the righteous into life eternal.

===========

Section - 1 - What happens to Christians.

===========

My advice to you, Is, Come to Jesus the Christ while you still can and live your life of love while you still can because if you do not, you will burn forever in a lake of fire and brimstone.

All that is being said here is believe in God the Father's son Jesus the Christ and try to live a sinless life, love one another and you will be saved.

Romans 8:1-2
1 There is therefore now no condemnation to them which are in Christ Jesus, who walk not after the flesh, but after the Spirit.
2 For the law of the Spirit of life in Christ Jesus hath made me free from the law of sin and death.

Do somthing for Jesus the Christ, Live your life of love, Love for God the Father, Jesus the Christ, Holy Spirit, yourself and your fellowman.

What happens to all Christian's, this scripture is the foundation of the Christian faith, please do something to show your love for God the Father, Jesus the Christ, the saints, your fellow men and yourself.

some examples is: giving money in church, give as much or as little as you want because God the Father loves a cheerful giver, volunteering with a charity or help them financially or do both, etc

1 Corinthians 3:11-15
11 For other foundation can no man lay than that is laid, which is Jesus Christ.
12 Now if any man build upon this foundation gold, silver, precious stones, wood, hay, stubble;
13 Every man's work shall be made manifest: for the day shall declare it, because it shall be revealed by fire; and the fire shall try every man's work of what sort it is.
14 If any man's work abide which he hath built thereupon, he shall receive a reward.
15 If any man's work shall be burned, he shall suffer loss: but he himself shall be saved; yet so as by fire.   Christian's will remain safely and peacefully with God the Father, Jesus the Christ, The Holy Spirit and the saved one's, Forever, Amen.

You are holy.
1 Corinthians 3:16-17
16 Know ye not that ye are the temple of God, and that the Spirit of God dwelleth in you?
17 If any man defile the temple of God, him shall God destroy; for the temple of God is holy, which temple ye are.
Return or come back to Jesus the Christ and be healed in every way.Living a loving life is the answer, Live your loving life.

   The prayer that people return to God the Father Jesus the Christ and the Holy Spirit if they left.

I ask that you say this prayer.
God the Father Please guide the people back to you Jesus the Christ and the Holy Spirit if they left, This I humbly ask in Jesus the Christ Holy name, Amen.

Scriptual bases.
The healing, Showing Jesus answer requests.Matthew 8:13
13 And Jesus said unto the centurion, Go thy way; and as thou hast believed, so be it done unto thee. And his servant was healed in the selfsame hour.What so ever ye ask in Jesus name, shall be done.

Mark 11:23-25
23 For verily I say unto you, That whosoever shall say unto this mountain, Be thou removed, and be thou cast into the sea; and shall not doubt in his heart, but shall believe that those things which he saith shall come to pass; he shall have whatsoever he saith.
24 Therefore I say unto you, What things soever ye desire, when ye pray, believe that ye receive them, and ye shall have them.
25 And when ye stand praying, forgive, if ye have ought against any: that your Father also which is in heaven may forgive you your trespasses.

Another example of comming back to God the Father in some of this parable Jesus tells.
Luke 15:20-32
20 And he arose, and came to his father. But when he was yet a great way off, his father saw him, and had compassion, and ran, and fell on his neck, and kissed him.
21 And the son said unto him, Father, I have sinned against heaven, and in thy sight, and am no more worthy to be called thy son.
22 But the father said to his servants, Bring forth the best robe, and put it on him; and put a ring on his hand, and shoes on his feet:
23 And bring hither the fatted calf, and kill it; and let us eat, and be merry:
24 For this my son was dead, and is alive again; he was lost, and is found.

And they began to be merry.

25 Now his elder son was in the field: and as he came and drew nigh to the house, he heard musick and dancing.

26 And he called one of the servants, and asked what these things meant.

27 And he said unto him, Thy brother is come; and thy father hath killed the fatted calf, because he hath received him safe and sound.

28 And he was angry, and would not go in: therefore came his father out, and intreated him.

29 And he answering said to his father, Lo, these many years do I serve thee, neither transgressed I at any time thy commandment: and yet thou never gavest me a kid, that I might make merry with my friends:

30 But as soon as this thy son was come, which hath devoured thy living with harlots, thou hast killed for him the fatted calf.

31 And he said unto him, Son, thou art ever with me, and all that I have is thine.

32 It was meet that we should make merry, and be glad: for this thy brother was dead, and is alive again; and was lost, and is found.

If you see something repeated in this book, it is because that is the way, God the Father had me put this book together.

============

Section - 2 - Confession of faith, get baptized.

============

Confession of Faith - If you haven't accepted Jesus or if you need to come back to Jesus say these word's: Jesus I believe that You are the Son of God, Jesus I believe that You came down here to earth as a man, Jesus I believe that You died for my sins (Wrong doings) and all of mankind sins, I believe that God Your Father raised You up from the dead and Jesus I believe that You went up into Heaven to be with Your Father, So that we can be forgiven of our sins, Jesus I confess that You are Lord and God and Jesus please forgive me of my sins and accept me into your family, Jesus I believe that You are coming back again for me one day. Amen.

Find a church and get baptized.

Find a church that agree with this document.
Share your faith with your fellowmen by encouraging them to become a Christian and tell them about this website.

==========

section - 3 - In the family of God the Father.

==========

"Being in the Family of God the Father."

Note: The big "G" in God is referring to God the Father and the little "g" in god is referring to every Christian even Jesus the Christ our Brother.

The Spirit of God is the Holy Ghost.
Joel 2:28
28 And it shall come to pass afterward, that I will pour out my spirit upon all flesh; and your sons and your daughters shall prophesy, your old men shall dream dreams, your young men shall see visions:

Romans 8:14-16
14 For as many as are led by the Spirit of God, they are the sons of God.
15 For ye have not received the spirit of bondage again to fear; but ye have received the Spirit of adoption, whereby we cry, Abba, Father.
16 The Spirit itself beareth witness with our spirit, that we are the children of God:

Romans 5:5
5 And hope maketh not ashamed; because the love of God is shed abroad in our hearts by the Holy Ghost which is given unto us.
All of God's Children are part of God and part of Man.

(God the Father) - (Jesus the Christ - the First Born Son of God the Father) - (The Holy Spirit - our Comforter) - (Say your name here because we are also God the Father sons and daughters)

We are included because we are God the Father's Children.

We will always be part of God and part of Man with the Holy Ghost as our comforter.

The Holy Ghost within us is what makes us part of God and part of Man.

Remember Jesus is the first born Son of God (The first to be risen from the dead by God) and we are his brother's and his sister's and we are all God's Children.

While Jesus was on the earth He was part of God and part of Man and he still is.

What made Him that way is found in Luke 1:35
Luke 1:35
35 And the angel answered and said unto her, The Holy Ghost shall come upon thee, and the power of the Highest shall overshadow thee: therefore also that holy thing which shall be born of thee shall be called the Son of God.

Because the Holy Ghost is within Jesus and because Mary berthed him, Jesus is forever part of God and part of Man.

To prove this, After Jesus was risen from the dead he appeared to his disciples being part of God and part of Man, Doing miracles.

Jesus appearing part of God and part of Man.
Luke 24:36-40
36 And as they thus spake, Jesus himself stood in the midst of them, and saith unto them, Peace be unto you.
37 But they were terrified and affrighted, and supposed that they had seen a spirit.
38 And he said unto them, Why are ye troubled? and why do thoughts

arise in your hearts?

39 Behold my hands and my feet, that it is I myself: handle me, and see; for a spirit hath not flesh and bones, as ye see me have.

40 And when he had thus spoken, he shewed them his hands and his feet.

Jesus Doing miracles.

St John 21:4-6

4 But when the morning was now come, Jesus stood on the shore: but the disciples knew not that it was Jesus.

5 Then Jesus saith unto them, Children, have ye any meat? They answered him, No.

6 And he said unto them, Cast the net on the right side of the ship, and ye shall find. They cast therefore, and now they were not able to draw it for the multitude of fishes.

The reason Jesus is called the Son of Man is because Mary birthed Him. How we become a child of God the Father is by becoming a Christian.

This is accomplished by believing upon Jesus the Christ and saying this statement : Jesus I believe that You are the Son of God, Jesus I believe that you were born from a virgin woman, Jesus I believe that You died for my sins and all of mankind sins, Jesus I confess that You are Lord and I believe that God Your Father raised You up from the dead and Jesus I believe that You went up into Heaven to be with Your Father Jesus I believe that You are coming back again for me one day, Amen

Next is to get baptized and to receive the Holy Ghost. So again if you have not been baptized, please do so.

The Holy Ghost Is what makes us part of God and because we were born of a woman we are also part of Man.

Jesus the Christ tried to tell people That they also are part of God and part of Man and they almost stoned him for it.

St John 10:22-39

22 And it was at Jerusalem the feast of the dedication, and it was winter.
23 And Jesus walked in the temple in Solomon's porch.
24 Then came the Jews round about him, and said unto him, How long dost thou make us to doubt? If thou be the Christ, tell us plainly.
25 Jesus answered them, I told you, and ye believed not: the works that I do in my Father's name, they bear witness of me.
26 But ye believe not, because ye are not of my sheep, as I said unto you.
27 My sheep hear my voice, and I know them, and they follow me:
28 And I give unto them eternal life; and they shall never perish, neither shall any man pluck them out of my hand.
29 My Father, which gave them me, is greater than all; and no man is able to pluck them out of my Father's hand.
30 I and my Father are one.Note: Jesus is saying that God is with him.
31 Then the Jews took up stones again to stone him.
32 Jesus answered them, Many good works have I shewed you from my Father; for which of those works do ye stone me?
33 The Jews answered him, saying, For a good work we stone thee not; but for blasphemy; and because that thou, being a man, makest thyself God.
34 Jesus answered them, Is it not written in your law, I said, Ye are gods?Note: Jesus is saying to the People that they also are Gods Children (part of God and part of Man).
35 If he called them gods, unto whom the word of God came, and the scripture cannot be broken;
36 Say ye of him, whom the Father hath sanctified, and sent into the world, Thou blasphemest; because I said, I am the Son of God?
37 If I do not the works of my Father, believe me not.
38 But if I do, though ye believe not me, believe the works: that ye may know, and believe, that the Father is in me, and I in him.

Note: Again Jesus is saying that God is with him.

39 Therefore they sought again to take him: but he escaped out of their

hand,
Jesus demonstrated some or all of the gifts of the Holy Ghost which proves he has the Holy Ghost and that he is part of God and part of Man.

About the gifts.
1 Corinthians 12:1-11
1 Now concerning spiritual gifts, brethren, I would not have you ignorant.
2 Ye know that ye were Gentiles, carried away unto these dumb idols, even as ye were led.
3 Wherefore I give you to understand, that no man speaking by the Spirit of God calleth Jesus accursed: and that no man can say that Jesus is the Lord, but by the Holy Ghost.
4 Now there are diversities of gifts, but the same Spirit.
5 And there are differences of administrations, but the same Lord.
6 And there are diversities of operations, but it is the same God which worketh all in all.
7 But the manifestation of the Spirit is given to every man to profit withal.
8 For to one is given by the Spirit the word of wisdom; to another the word of knowledge by the same Spirit;
9 To another faith by the same Spirit; to another the gifts of healing by the same Spirit;
10 To another the working of miracles; to another prophecy; to another discerning of spirits; to another divers kinds of tongues; to another the of tongues:
11 But all these worketh that one and the selfsame Spirit, dividing to every man severally as he will.

Note: I encourage you to find out the gift or gifts you have and use them, Just as Jesus did.
Jesus Said
St John 14:12
12 Verily, verily, I say unto you, He that believeth on me, the works that I do shall he do also; and greater works than these shall he do; because I go unto my Father.

You may ask - well What about where God called Jesus God with a capital "G", and where it says Jesus sits on Gods Throne with God ?.

Remember God with a capital "G" is referring to God the Father.

Jesus being called God with a capital "G".
Hebrews 1:8
8 But unto the Son he saith, Thy throne, O God, is for ever and ever: a sceptre of righteousness is the sceptre of thy kingdom.

Sharing Jesus throne, Jesus sharing Gods throne.
Revelations 3:21
21 To him that overcometh will I grant to sit with me in my throne, even as I also overcame, and am set down with my Father in his throne.

Just like Jesus shared Gods throne, We shall share Jesus throne.
God was sharing his throne with his son Jesus the Christ when he said "O God" with a capital "G", God may not share his throne with us, But we do know that we shall share Jesus throne if we qualify to receive eternal life.

Jesus still remain Jesus the Christ whenever he share's God the Father's throne just as we remain ourselves if we are saved and share Jesus the Christ throne.

I think one of the reasons God shared his throne with Jesus is because he was glad to have his son with him and remember God and Jesus created the heavens and the earth and everything in it together and Jesus worked with God to save mankind from destruction, All we have to do to be saved is believe on Jesus the Christ and live a life of love.

So even though we may not qualify to share Gods throne we do qualify to share Jesus throne if we receive eternal life.

I encourage you to strive to live such a life as to qualify to receive eternal life and to share Jesus the Christ throne.

Remember God is our Father and Jesus is our Brother and we all are one big family.

Note: I have heard people say that Jesus was beaten to the point that a person could not recognize him when he was crucified, This is not true, To prove this, his disciples recognized him when he appeared to them after God rose him up from the dead.

Jesus appearing part of God and part of Man.
Luke 24:36-40
36 And as they thus spake, Jesus himself stood in the midst of them, and saith unto them, Peace be unto you.
37 But they were terrified and affrighted, and supposed that they had seen a spirit.
38 And he said unto them, Why are ye troubled? and why do thoughts arise in your hearts?
39 Behold my hands and my feet, that it is I myself: handle me, and see; for a spirit hath not flesh and bones, as ye see me have.
40 And when he had thus spoken, he shewed them his hands and his feet.
==========

section - 4 - Warning's about your enemy the devil, (satan). Understand this, the devil is real. Do not doubt this. He wants to see you burn forever with him. try not to let this happen. There is only salvation in Jesus the Christ. Come to Jesus, God the Father son, if you have not.
==========

    Scripture's about your enemy the devil and how much he hate's you and how much God the Father, Jesus the Christ and the Holy Spirit loves you,
----
2 Timothy 2:26
26 and that they will come to their senses and escape from the trap of the devil, who has taken them captive to do his will.

One of the tools the devil uses, Is to play mind games with you to get you to hurt yourself or somebody else, DO NOT FALL FOR IT, I fell for one of his lies, and I hope no one was hurt permanently, If anyone was hurt, I already prayed for a swift recovery for that person and I already asked God the Father for forgiveness, In Jesus the Christ Holy name and I believe I am forgiven, I am continuing my Christian journey of love, You can also ask God for forgiveness and continue your journey of love, Remember, Loving other's is loving yourself.

What happened, is I would not talk to this man on the bus, I was on, about my booklet.

God love's you and will work with you for a good out come, Just like he love's me and is working with me for a good out come.

If you feel that you failed God the Father, Jesus the Christ and the Holy Spirit in a big way, Don't worry, Stay with them anyway and believe and serve them anyway, For we all should strive for perfection, God the Father, Jesus the Christ and the Holy Spirit already won the battle against the devil also known as satan,angel of light,day star,roaring lion, lucifer, these are some of his name's.

Looking to God the Father and Jesus the Christ and the Holy Spirit and the warning Jesus tells us about the devil.
1 Peter 5:6-11
6 Humble yourselves therefore under the mighty hand of God, that he may exalt you in due time:
7 Casting all your care upon him; for he careth for you.
8 Be sober, be vigilant; because your adversary the devil, as a roaring lion, walketh about, seeking whom he may devour:
9 Whom resist stedfast in the faith, knowing that the same afflictions are accomplished in your brethren that are in the world.
10 But the God of all grace, who hath called us unto his eternal glory by

Christ Jesus, after that ye have suffered a while, make you perfect, stablish, strengthen, settle you.11 To him be glory and dominion for ever and ever. Amen.

Ephesian 6:11-18Put on the whole armour of God.

11 Put on the whole armour of God, that ye may be able to stand against the wiles of the devil.

12 For we wrestle not against flesh and blood, but against principalities, against powers, against the rulers of the darkness of this world, against spiritual wickedness in high places.

13 Wherefore take unto you the whole armour of God, that ye may be able to withstand in the evil day, and having done all, to stand.

14 Stand therefore, having your loins girt about with truth, and having on the breastplate of righteousness;

15 And your feet shod with the preparation of the gospel of peace;

16 Above all, taking the shield of faith, wherewith ye shall be able to quench all the fiery darts of the wicked.

17 And take the helmet of salvation, and the sword of the Spirit, which is the word of God:

18 Praying always with all prayer and supplication in the Spirit, and watching thereunto with all perseverance and supplication for all saints;s.

Jesus is the only way to salvation, he destroys the works of the devil, John 10:9-11

9 I am the door: by me if any man enter in, he shall be saved, and shall go in and out, and find pasture.

10 The thief cometh not, but for to steal, and to kill, and to destroy: I am come that they might have life, and that they might have it more abundantly.

11 I am the good shepherd: the good shepherd giveth his life for the sheep.and now he forever live's

----

Be righteous
1 John 3:7-9

7 Little children, let no man deceive you: he that doeth righteousness is righteous, even as he is righteous.
8 He that committeth sin is of the devil; for the devil sinneth from the beginning. For this purpose the Son of God was manifested, that he might destroy the works of the devil.
9 Whosoever is born of God doth not commit sin; for his seed remaineth in him: and he cannot sin, because he is born of God.

Resist the devil and he will flee.
James 4:7
7Submit yourselves therefore to God. Resist the devil, and he will flee from you.

Again: One of the tools the devil uses, Is to play mind games with you to get you to hurt yourself or somebody else, DO NOT FALL FOR IT, I fell for one of his lies, and I hope no one was hurt permanently, If anyone was hurt, I already prayed for a swift recovery for that person and I already asked God the Father for forgiveness, In Jesus the Christ Holy name and I believe I am forgiven, I am continuing my Christian journey of love, You can also ask God for forgiveness and continue your journey of love, Remember, Loving other's is loving yourself.

What happened, is I would not talk to this man on the bus, I was on, about my booklet.
    God love's you and will work with you for a good out come, Just like he love's me and is working with me for a good out come.

If you feel that you failed God the Father, Jesus the Christ and the Holy Spirit in a big way, Don't worry, Stay with them anyway and believe and serve them anyway, For we all should strive for perfection, God the Father, Jesus the Christ and the Holy Spirit already won the battle against the devil also known as satan.

One of the things the devil (Gods enemy) does is try to make you think that things are more worse than they really are, and it's just not.

The devil's fate.
Revelation 20:10
10 And the devil that deceived them was cast into the lake of fire and brimstone, where the beast and the false prophet are, and shall be tormented day and night for ever and ever.

This is the end of my warnings about the devil (satan),your enemy.
==========

section - 5 - Listing of sins, that if you are doing, you need to confess and turn away from, if you fail to turn away from that or those sins, try again, and if you keep failing keep trying, do not give up.
==========

Beware of pride - It is often considered the opposite of shame or of humility.

Beware of vanity - Being to proud of yourself or your achievements, Vanity is an enemy of the Spirit and must be constantly brought to the cross and crucified.

Try to stay humble - Understanding the biblical meaning of "humble" is essential for anyone seeking to deepen their faith and practice. It invites us to reflect on our attitudes, challenge our pride, and embrace a lifestyle rooted in servanthood and love. As we strive to embody humility, we align ourselves with the teachings of Jesus and the heart of God, ultimately leading to a more fulfilling and purposeful spiritual journey.

God the Father hates sins so much, he destroyed every one on the planet, except, eight people in the great flood, consider this as you read.

Genesis 6:11-13
11 The earth also was corrupt before God, and the earth was filled with violence.
12 And God looked upon the earth, and, behold, it was corrupt; for all

flesh had corrupted his way upon the earth.
13 And God said unto Noah, The end of all flesh is come before me; for the earth is filled with violence through them; and, behold, I will destroy them with the earth.

Repenting of sins.   Saving others is saving yourself.
James 5:19-20
19 My brothers and sisters, if one of you should wander from the truth and someone should bring that person back,
20 remember this: Whoever turns a sinner from the error of their way will save them from death and cover over a multitude of sins.

Try to live a sinless life. If you fail, try again. We all should strive for perfection, even if we fall short of it sometimes.

The eyes is the key to the body and we should be careful about what we see.
Matthew 6:21-23
21 For where your treasure is, there your heart will be also.
22 The eye is the lamp of the body. If your eyes are healthy, your whole body will be full of light.
23 But if your eyes are unhealthy, your whole body will be full of darkness. If then the light within you is darkness, how great is that darkness!
Matthew 5:29
29 And if thy right eye offend thee, pluck it out, and cast it from thee: for it is profitable for thee that one of thy members should perish, and not that thy whole body should be cast into hell.

1 Corinthians 6:18-20
18 Flee from sexual immorality. All other sins a person commits are outside the body, but whoever sins sexually, sins against their own body.
19 Do you not know that your bodies are temples of the Holy Spirit, who is in you, whom you have received from God? You are not your own;

20 you were bought at a price. Therefore honor God with your bodies.   All that is being said here is believe in God the Father's son Jesus the Christ and try to live a sinless life, love one another and you will be saved.

I strongly ask that you stop watching television shows and movies, throw out your DVDs, and try to be careful of the music you listen to and the books you read.   they can send a worldly message.   Meaning: They promote all kinds of sins. Do this for your own good   Remember the Holy Spirit of God the Father is doing it right alone with you, what ever you are doing, try not to grieve it.
If you discover that you are grieving the Holy Spirit, stop what you are doing and ask for forgiveness.

I am stressing this point to you because it is very important, God the Father, Jesus the Christ, the Holy Spirit and the saints, hates sins and they expect for us to hate sins as well.

There is a strong possibility that you might get severely punished by God the Father for watching television shows and movies and playing video games promoting all sorts of sins it, throw out your DVDs and video games, and try to be careful of the music you listen to and the books you read, Take this seriously.

If it starts to change your morals, for the worse, stop it, This is all about cleaning yourself up for yourself and your creators.

There is also the possibility that you may or may not get demon oppressed by watching certain movies, television shows, reading books, and playing video games or playing certain music with all sorts of sins in excess. Please leave those things alone, for your own good.   Do something positive with your time.

Check out this website about stop watching television.

Top 10 Reasons You Should Stop Watching TV - https://personalexcellence.co/blog/stop-watching-tv/

The prayer: God the Father, please free me from any demon that may tempt me or oppress me, this I humbly ask in Jesus Christ Holy name. Amen.

If God the Father frees you, try not to go back into what you were doing. Keep trying until you are free. Do not give up. If you are sinning, you need to confess and ask God the Father for forgiveness and turn away from those sins; if you fail to turn away from those sins, try again and if you keep failing, keep trying. Do not give up.

A list of the sins (Wrong doing) that if you are doing, you need to turn away from and ask God for forgiveness in Jesus name, some sins are, Idolatry - Putting anything or person in the place of God the Father the creator, murder, abortion, lesbianism Romans 1:26, homosexuality Romans 1:27, adultery, masturbation, fighting and doing illegal drugs.

God the Father, ten Commandments in order,
Exodus 20:1-17   I am the Lord your God.   You shall worship no other gods beside me.   You shall not carry God's name in vain.   Remember the Sabbath day to keep it holy.   Honor your father and mother.   You shall not murder.   You shall not commit adultery.   You shall not steal.   You shall not bear false witness against your neighbor.   You shall not covet your neighbor's house: you shall not covet your neighbor's wife Or anything that is your neighbor's.

Note: To the churches and schools. Post, read, pass out copies to church members and to the public and talk about these sins and the ten commandments, often.

God loves mankind, Satan hates mankind, Be on Gods side.

What Jesus says about fighting and revenge.
Matthew 5:38-39
38 You have heard that it was said, Eye for eye, and tooth for tooth.
39 But I tell you, do not resist an evil person. If anyone slaps you on the right cheek, turn to them the other cheek also.

About revenge.
Romans 12:19
19 Do not take revenge, my dear friends, but leave room for God's wrath, for it is written: It is mine to avenge; I will repay, says the Lord.
===========

section - 6 - Love yourself enough, to not stop your christen life of love, do not give up, remember loving others is loving yourself.
===========

Love yourself enough, to not stop your christen life of love, do not give up, remember loving others is loving yourself.

Matthew 25:31-46
31 When the Son of man shall come in his glory, and all the holy angels with him, then shall he sit upon the throne of his glory:
32 And before him shall be gathered all nations: and he shall separate them one from another, as a shepherd divideth his sheep from the goats:
33 And he shall set the sheep on his right hand, but the goats on the left.
34 Then shall the King say unto them on his right hand, Come, ye blessed of my Father, inherit the kingdom prepared for you from the foundation of the world:
35 For I was an hungred, and ye gave me meat: I was thirsty, and ye gave me drink: I was a stranger, and ye took me in:
36 Naked, and ye clothed me: I was sick, and ye visited me: I was in prison, and ye came unto me.
37 Then shall the righteous answer him, saying, Lord, when saw we thee an hungred, and fed thee? or thirsty, and gave thee drink?

38 When saw we thee a stranger, and took thee in? or naked, and clothed thee?

39 Or when saw we thee sick, or in prison, and came unto thee?

40 And the King shall answer and say unto them, Verily I say unto you, Inasmuch as ye have done it unto one of the least of these my brethren, ye have done it unto me.

41 Then shall he say also unto them on the left hand, Depart from me, ye cursed, into everlasting fire, prepared for the devil and his angels:

42 For I was an hungred, and ye gave me no meat: I was thirsty, and ye gave me no drink:

43 I was a stranger, and ye took me not in: naked, and ye clothed me not: sick, and in prison, and ye visited me not.

44 Then shall they also answer him, saying, Lord, when saw we thee an hungred, or athirst, or a stranger, or naked, or sick, or in prison, and did not minister unto thee?

45 Then shall he answer them, saying, Verily I say unto you, Inasmuch as ye did it not to one of the least of these, ye did it not to me.

46 And these shall go away into everlasting punishment: but the righteous into life eternal.

Endure unto the end.

Luke 21:7-19

7 And they asked him, saying, Master, but when shall these things be? and what sign will there be when these things shall come to pass?

8 And he said, Take heed that ye be not deceived: for many shall come in my name, saying, I am Christ; and the time draweth near: go ye not therefore after them.

9 But when ye shall hear of wars and commotions, be not terrified: for these things must first come to pass; but the end is not by and by.

10 Then said he unto them, Nation shall rise against nation, and kingdom against kingdom:

11 And great earthquakes shall be in divers places, and famines, and pestilences; and fearful sights and great signs shall there be from heaven.

12 But before all these, they shall lay their hands on you, and persecute

you, delivering you up to the synagogues, and into prisons, being brought before kings and rulers for my name's sake.

13 And it shall turn to you for a testimony.

14 Settle it therefore in your hearts, not to meditate before what ye shall answer:

15 For I will give you a mouth and wisdom, which all your adversaries shall not be able to gainsay nor resist.

16 And ye shall be betrayed both by parents, and brethren, and kinsfolks, and friends; and some of you shall they cause to be put to death.

17 And ye shall be hated of all men for my name's sake.

18 But there shall not an hair of your head perish.

19 In your patience possess ye your souls.

==========

section - 7 - Look to God the Father Son, Jesus the Christ, just like I am, to be saved, Because there is only salvation through him.

==========

Look to God the Father son, Jesus the Christ, just like I am, to be saved, Because there is only salvation through him.

Jesus say's.
John 14:6
6 Jesus saith unto him, I am the way, the truth, and the life: no man cometh unto the Father, but by me.

==========

section - 8 - Build or continue your relation with God the Father, Jesus the Christ, The Holy Sprit and the saints.

==========

Build or continue your relation with God the Father, Jesus the Christ, The Holy Sprit and the saints.

Matthew 22:36-40

36 Master, which is the great commandment in the law?

37 Jesus said unto him, Thou shalt love the Lord thy God with all thy heart, and with all thy soul, and with all thy mind.

38 This is the first and great commandment.

39 And the second is like unto it, Thou shalt love thy neighbour as thyself.
40 On these two commandments hang all the law and the prophets.

If you love the lord your God with all your heart and with all your soul, and with all your mind and if you love your neighbor as yourself you will not want to do anything against God, and also you will not want to do anything against your neighbor, This is how we fulfill the law.

That is why Jesus said in (Matthew 22:40) On these two commandments hang all the law and the prophets.

And also in (Galations 5:14) further confirms Jesus statement.
14 For all the law is fulfilled in one word, even in this; Thou shalt love thy neighbour as thyself

===========

section - 9 - Diffarent subjects to study, to help you understand the Holy Bible more.

===========

The Person of Christ.
Colossians 1:15-23
15 Who is the image of the invisible God, the firstborn of every creature:
16 For by him were all things created, that are in heaven, and that are in earth, visible and invisible, whether they be thrones, or dominions, or principalities, or powers: all things were created by him, and for him:
17 And he is before all things, and by him all things consist.
18 And he is the head of the body, the church: who is the beginning, the firstborn from the dead; that in all things he might have the preeminence.
19 For it pleased the Father that in him should all fulness dwell;
20 And, having made peace through the blood of his cross, by him to reconcile all things unto himself; by him, I say, whether they be things in earth, or things in heaven.
21 And you, that were sometime alienated and enemies in your mind by wicked works, yet now hath he reconciled
22 In the body of his flesh through death, to present you holy and

unblameable and unreproveable in his sight:

23 If ye continue in the faith grounded and settled, and be not moved away from the hope of the gospel, which ye have heard, and which was preached to every creature which is under heaven; whereof I Paul am made a minister;

Ephesians 1:3-14

3 Blessed be the God and Father of our Lord Jesus Christ, who hath blessed us with all spiritual blessings in heavenly places in Christ:

4 According as he hath chosen us in him before the foundation of the world, that we should be holy and without blame before him in love:

5 Having predestinated us unto the adoption of children by Jesus Christ to himself, according to the good pleasure of his will,

6 To the praise of the glory of his grace, wherein he hath made us accepted in the beloved.

7 In whom we have redemption through his blood, the forgiveness of sins, according to the riches of his grace;

8 Wherein he hath abounded toward us in all wisdom and prudence;

9 Having made known unto us the mystery of his will, according to his good pleasure which he hath purposed in himself:

10 That in the dispensation of the fulness of times he might gather together in one all things in Christ, both which are in heaven, and which are on earth; even in him:

11 In whom also we have obtained an inheritance, being predestinated according to the purpose of him who worketh all things after the counsel of his own will:

12 That we should be to the praise of his glory, who first trusted in Christ.

13 In whom ye also trusted, after that ye heard the word of truth, the gospel of your salvation: in whom also after that ye believed, ye were sealed with that holy Spirit of promise,

14 Which is the earnest of our inheritance until the redemption of the purchased possession, unto the praise of his glory.

Romans 8:28-31

28 And we know that all things work together for good to them that love God, to them who are the called according to his purpose.
29 For whom he did foreknow, he also did predestinate to be conformed to the image of his Son, that he might be the firstborn among many brethren.
30 Moreover whom he did predestinate, them he also called: and whom he called, them he also justified: and whom he justified, them he also glorified.
31 What shall we then say to these things? If God be for us, who can be against us?

Question: Who are the predestinated, Called, Justified and Glorified. Answer: The answer is found in (St John 3:16-18) - (Romans 10:9-13)

John 3:16-18
16 For God so loved the world, that he gave his only begotten Son, that whosoever believeth in him should not perish, but have everlasting life.
17 For God sent not his Son into the world to condemn the world; but that the world through him might be saved.
18 He that believeth on him is not condemned: but he that believeth not is condemned already, because he hath not believed in the name of the only begotten Son of God.

Romans 10:9-13
9 That if thou shalt confess with thy mouth the Lord Jesus, and shalt believe in thine heart that God hath raised him from the dead, thou shalt be saved.
10 For with the heart man believeth unto righteousness; and with the mouth confession is made unto salvation.
11 For the scripture saith, Whosoever believeth on him shall not be ashamed.
12 For there is no difference between the Jew and the Greek: for the same Lord over all is rich unto all that call upon him.
13 For whosoever shall call upon the name of the Lord shall be saved.

----

1 John 1:5-10

5 This then is the message which we have heard of him, and declare unto you, that God is light, and in him is no darkness at all.

6 If we say that we have fellowship with him, and walk in darkness, we lie, and do not the truth:

7 But if we walk in the light, as he is in the light, we have fellowship one with another, and the blood of Jesus Christ his Son cleanseth us from all sin.

8 If we say that we have no sin, we deceive ourselves, and the truth is not in us.

9 If we confess our sins, he is faithful and just to forgive us our sins, and to cleanse us from all unrighteousness.

10 If we say that we have not sinned, we make him a liar, and his word is not in us.

THE PRAYER FOR FORGIVENESS

Father God in heaven.Even though I strive to live a sin free life, I know I probably have not.

Please forgive me any sins that I have done.This I humbly ask in Jesus Holy name, Amen.

Ephesians 2:4-10

4 But God, who is rich in mercy, for his great love wherewith he loved us,

5 Even when we were dead in sins, hath quickened us together with Christ, (by grace ye are saved;)

6 And hath raised us up together, and made us sit together in heavenly places in Christ Jesus:

7 That in the ages to come he might shew the exceeding riches of his grace in his kindness toward us through Christ Jesus.

8 For by grace are ye saved through faith; and that not of yourselves: it is the gift of God:

9 Not of works, lest any man should boast.
10 For we are his workmanship, created in Christ Jesus unto good works, which God hath before ordained that we should walk in them.

Right with God
Romans 5:1-11
1 Therefore being justified by faith, we have peace with God through our Lord Jesus Christ:
2 By whom also we have access by faith into this grace wherein we stand, and rejoice in hope of the glory of God.
3 And not only so, but we glory in tribulations also: knowing that tribulation worketh patience;
4 And patience, experience; and experience, hope:
5 And hope maketh not ashamed; because the love of God is shed abroad in our hearts by the Holy Ghost which is given unto us.
6 For when we were yet without strength, in due time Christ died for the ungodly.
7 For scarcely for a righteous man will one die: yet peradventure for a good man some would even dare to die.
8 But God commendeth his love toward us, in that, while we were yet sinners, Christ died for us.
9 Much more then, being now justified by his blood, we shall be saved from wrath through him.
10 For if, when we were enemies, we were reconciled to God by the death of his Son, much more, being reconciled, we shall be saved by his life.
11 And not only so, but we also joy in God through our Lord Jesus Christ, by whom we have now received the atonement.

How God put us right with him.
Romans 3:21-26
21 But now the righteousness of God without the law is manifested, being witnessed by the law and the prophets;
22 Even the righteousness of God which is by faith of Jesus Christ unto all and upon all them that believe: for there is no difference:

23 For all have sinned, and come short of the glory of God;
24 Being justified freely by his grace through the redemption that is in Christ Jesus:
25 Whom God hath set forth to be a propitiation through faith in his blood, to declare his righteousness for the remission of sins that are past, through the forbearance of God;
26 To declare, I say, at this time his righteousness: that he might be just, and the justifier of him which believeth in Jesus.

Hebrews 10:1-18
1 For the law having a shadow of good things to come, and not the very image of the things, can never with those sacrifices which they offered year by year continually make the comers thereunto perfect.
2 For then would they not have ceased to be offered? because that the worshippers once purged should have had no more conscience of sins.
3 But in those sacrifices there is a remembrance again made of sins every year.
4 For it is not possible that the blood of bulls and of goats should take away sins.
5 Wherefore when he cometh into the world, he saith, Sacrifice and offering thou wouldest not, but a body hast thou prepared me:
6 In burnt offerings and sacrifices for sin thou hast had no pleasure.
7 Then said I, Lo, I come (in the volume of the book it is written of me,) to do thy will, O God.
8 Above when he said, Sacrifice and offering and burnt offerings and offering for sin thou wouldest not, neither hadst pleasure therein; which are offered by the law;
9 Then said he, Lo, I come to do thy will, O God. He taketh away the first, that he may establish the second.
10 By the which will we are sanctified through the offering of the body of Jesus Christ once for all.
11 And every priest standeth daily ministering and offering oftentimes the same sacrifices, which can never take away sins:
12 But this man, after he had offered one sacrifice for sins for ever, sat

down on the right hand of God;

13 From henceforth expecting till his enemies be made his footstool.

14 For by one offering he hath perfected for ever them that are sanctified.

15 Whereof the Holy Ghost also is a witness to us: for after that he had said before,

16 This is the covenant that I will make with them after those days, saith the Lord, I will put my laws into their hearts, and in their minds will I write them;

17 And their sins and iniquities will I remember no more.

18 Now where remission of these is, there is no more offering for sin.

Hebrews 13:20-21

20 Now the God of peace, that brought again from the dead our Lord Jesus, that great shepherd of the sheep, through the blood of the everlasting covenant,

21 Make you perfect in every good work to do his will, working in you that which is wellpleasing in his sight, through Jesus Christ; to whom be glory for ever and ever. Amen.

Part 2
Lord, Lord
Matthew 7:13-14

13 Enter ye in at the strait gate: for wide is the gate, and broad is the way, that leadeth to destruction, and many there be which go in thereat:

14 Because strait is the gate, and narrow is the way, which leadeth unto life, and few there be that find it.

Matthew 7:21-23

21 Not every one that saith unto me, Lord, Lord, shall enter into the kingdom of heaven; but he that doeth the will of my Father which is in heaven.

22 Many will say to me in that day, Lord, Lord, have we not prophesied in thy name? and in thy name have cast out devils? and in thy name done many wonderful works?

23 And then will I profess unto them, I never knew you: depart from me, ye that work iniquity.

Question: what is the will of the Father (God), Which Jesus is talking about in "(Matthew 7:21).

Answer: The will of the Father (God), Is the same as Jesus will, Jesus tells us what the will of the Father (God) is in the Parables he tells us and also the other things he teaches and tells us, and also what Jesus disciples teaches us.

Question: Why did Jesus say in (Matthew 7:21) Not every one that saith unto me, Lord, Lord, shall enter into the kingdom of heaven;

Answer: The answer is found in (Matthew 7:23) Jesus is speaking to the people that work iniquity.

Question: What is Iniquity.

Answer: The definition for the word iniquity is: 1 shameful Injustice: wickedness 2 an unjust or wicked act or thing.

Be wise, listen to Jesus.
Luke 6:46-49
46 And why call ye me, Lord, Lord, and do not the things which I say?
47 Whosoever cometh to me, and heareth my sayings, and doeth them, I will shew you to whom he is like:
48 He is like a man which built an house, and digged deep, and laid the foundation on a rock: and when the flood arose, the stream beat vehemently upon that house, and could not shake it: for it was founded upon a rock.
49 But he that heareth, and doeth not, is like a man that without a foundation built an house upon the earth; against which the stream did beat vehemently, and immediately it fell; and the ruin of that house was great.

St John 14:23-24

23 Jesus answered and said unto him, If a man love me, he will keep my words: and my Father will love him, and we will come unto him, and make our abode with him.

24 He that loveth me not keepeth not my sayings: and the word which ye hear is not mine, but the Father's which sent me.

Part 3

Courage before God
1 John 3:19-24

19 And hereby we know that we are of the truth, and shall assure our hearts before him.

20 For if our heart condemn us, God is greater than our heart, and knoweth all things.

21 Beloved, if our heart condemn us not, then have we confidence toward God.

22 And whatsoever we ask, we receive of him, because we keep his commandments, and do those things that are pleasing in his sight.

23 And this is his commandment, That we should believe on the name of his Son Jesus Christ, and love one another, as he gave us commandment.

24 And he that keepeth his commandments dwelleth in him, and he in him. And hereby we know that he abideth in us, by the Spirit which he hath given us.

Come to Jesus if you have not, For now is the acceptable time.
John 3:16-18

16 For God so loved the world, that he gave his only begotten Son, that whosoever believeth in him should not perish, but have everlasting life.

17 For God sent not his Son into the world to condemn the world; but that the world through him might be saved.

18 He that believeth on him is not condemned: but he that believeth not is condemned already, because he hath not believed in the name of the only

begotten Son of God.

Believe in Jesus while you still can, While you still have a chance to, Jesus the Son of God is comming back again.

Romans 10:9-10
9 That if thou shalt confess with thy mouth the Lord Jesus, and shalt believe in thine heart that God hath raised him from the dead, thou shalt be saved.

So confess that Jesus is Lord and believe that God has raised him up from the dead, and you will be saved.

10 For with the heart man believeth unto righteousness; and with the mouth confession is made unto salvation.

Repent of your sins, Come to Jesus the Son of God, while you still have a chance.
Matthew 13:41-42
41 The Son of man shall send forth his angels, and they shall gather out of his kingdom all things that offend, and them which do iniquity;
42 And shall cast them into a furnace of fire: there shall be wailing and gnashing of teeth.
You don't have to be condemned to burn forever in the lake of fire and brimstone, Believe in Jesus the Son of God and turn from your wicked ways.

If you have not acceptted Jesus the Son of God the one that died for your sins. now is the time, don't let it be to late, believe in Jesus before it's to late.

If you have not been baptized in the name of the Father the Son and the Holy Ghost, Please go get baptized.

Fortify your position in Jesus the Christ.
the definition of the word fortify is -----To make strong: To strengthen and secure by military defences.

Realize that Jesus loves you.
John 3:16
16 For God so loved the world, that he gave his only begotten Son, that whosoever believeth in him should not perish, but have everlasting life.

Jesus loved you so much that he died for your sins, so you would not have to burn forever in that lake of fire and brimstone.

Now is the time of salvation, Don't let it be to late, Believe on Jesus while you still can.

Keep on doing good worksRomans 2:6-11
6 Who will render to every man according to his deeds:
7 To them who by patient continuance in well doing seek for glory and honour and immortality, eternal life:
8 But unto them that are contentious, and do not obey the truth, but obey unrighteousness, indignation and wrath,
9 Tribulation and anguish, upon every soul of man that doeth evil, of the Jew first, and also of the Gentile;
10 But glory, honour, and peace, to every man that worketh good, to the Jew first, and also to the Gentile:
11 For there is no respect of persons with God.

In the parable the sheeps and the goats, Jesus is showing how we should help one another.
By helping one another we show that we love God, Jesus, The Holy Ghost and our fellowmen, We also show that we are saved and that our faith is alive.

The sheep and the goats. * Jesus remembering your good deeds.

Matthew 25:31-46

31 When the Son of man shall come in his glory, and all the holy angels with him, then shall he sit upon the throne of his glory:

32 And before him shall be gathered all nations: and he shall separate them one from another, as a shepherd divideth his sheep from the goats:

33 And he shall set the sheep on his right hand, but the goats on the left.

34 Then shall the King say unto them on his right hand, Come, ye blessed of my Father, inherit the kingdom prepared for you from the foundation of the world:

35 For I was an hungred, and ye gave me meat: I was thirsty, and ye gave me drink: I was a stranger, and ye took me in:

36 Naked, and ye clothed me: I was sick, and ye visited me: I was in prison, and ye came unto me.

37 Then shall the righteous answer him, saying, Lord, when saw we thee an hungred, and fed thee? or thirsty, and gave thee drink?

38 When saw we thee a stranger, and took thee in? or naked, and clothed thee?

39 Or when saw we thee sick, or in prison, and came unto thee?

40 And the King shall answer and say unto them, Verily I say unto you, Inasmuch as ye have done it unto one of the least of these my brethren, ye have done it unto me.

41 Then shall he say also unto them on the left hand, Depart from me, ye cursed, into everlasting fire, prepared for the devil and his angels:

42 For I was an hungred, and ye gave me no meat: I was thirsty, and ye gave me no drink:

43 I was a stranger, and ye took me not in: naked, and ye clothed me not: sick, and in prison, and ye visited me not.

44 Then shall they also answer him, saying, Lord, when saw we thee an hungred, or athirst, or a stranger, or naked, or sick, or in prison, and did not minister unto thee?

45 Then shall he answer them, saying, Verily I say unto you, Inasmuch as ye did it not to one of the least of these, ye did it not to me.

46 And these shall go away into everlasting punishment: but the righteous into life eternal.

Alms Giving.
Matthew 6:1-4
1 Take heed that ye do not your alms before men, to be seen of them: otherwise ye have no reward of your Father which is in heaven.
2 Therefore when thou doest thine alms, do not sound a trumpet before thee, as the hypocrites do in the synagogues and in the streets, that they may have glory of men. Verily I say unto you, They have their reward.
3 But when thou
4 That thine alms may be in secret: and thy Father which seeth in secret himself shall reward thee openly.

Luke 6:38
38 Give, and it shall be given unto you; good measure, pressed down, and shaken together, and running over, shall men give into your bosom. For with the same measure that ye mete withal it shall be measured to you again.

Love in deed and in truth.1 John 3:17-18
17 But whoso hath this world's good, and seeth his brother have need, and shutteth up his bowels of compassion from him, how dwelleth the love of God in him?
18 My little children, let us not love in word, neither in tongue; but in deed and in truth.

James 1:22
22 But be ye doers of the word, and not hearers only, deceiving your own selves.

James 2:14-17
14 What doth it profit, my brethren, though a man say he hath faith, and have not works? can faith save him?
15 If a brother or sister be naked, and destitute of daily food,
16 And one of you say unto them, Depart in peace, be ye warmed and

filled; notwithstanding ye give them not those things which are needful to the body; what doth it profit?
17 Even so faith, if it hath not works, is dead, being alone.

As James said faith without works is dead, (James 2:17) James is refering to the work of the Holy Ghost and Jesus in his parable the sheeps and the Goats (Matthew 25:31-46) Illustrated the people who's faith is alive (Matthew 25:31-40) and the people who's faith is dead (Matthew 25:41-46).

The Parable of the good samaritanIn the parable Jesus tells about the good samaritan, Jesus is further illustrating the people who's faith is alive.

Luke 10:25-37
25 And, behold, a certain lawyer stood up, and tempted him, saying, Master, what shall I do to inherit eternal life?
26 He said unto him, What is written in the law? how readest thou?
27 And he answering said, Thou shalt love the Lord thy God with all thy heart, and with all thy soul, and with all thy strength, and with all thy mind; and thy neighbour as thyself.
28 And he said unto him, Thou hast answered right: this do, and thou shalt live.
29 But he, willing to justify himself, said unto Jesus, And who is my neighbour?
30 And Jesus answering said, A certain man went down from Jerusalem to Jericho, and fell among thieves, which stripped him of his raiment, and wounded him, and departed, leaving him half dead.
31 And by chance there came down a certain priest that way: and when he saw him, he passed by on the other side.
32 And likewise a Levite, when he was at the place, came and looked on him, and passed by on the other side.
33 But a certain Samaritan, as he journeyed, came where he was: and when he saw him, he had compassion on him,
34 And went to him, and bound up his wounds, pouring in oil and wine,

and set him on his own beast, and brought him to an inn, and took care of him.

35 And on the morrow when he departed, he took out two pence, and gave them to the host, and said unto him, Take care of him; and whatsoever thou spendest more, when I come again, I will repay thee.

36 Which now of these three, thinkest thou, was neighbour unto him that fell among the thieves?

37 And he said, He that shewed mercy on him. Then said Jesus unto him, Go, and do thou likewise.

Fulfilling the lawGod gave the israelites the law which is written in the old testament, The laws are written in the books of Exodus, Leviticus, Numbers, Gods laws consist of rules and regulations that the isaelites had to live by, When they did what was written in the law, They was doing what the law required of them to do, they did the works of the law.

How we all come under gods laws.Romans 2:11-16

11 For there is no respect of persons with God.

12 For as many as have sinned without law shall also perish without law: and as many as have sinned in the law shall be judged by the law;

13 (For not the hearers of the law are just before God, but the doers of the law shall be justified.

14 For when the Gentiles, which have not the law, do by nature the things contained in the law, these, having not the law, are a law unto themselves:

15 Which shew the work of the law written in their hearts, their conscience also bearing witness, and their thoughts the mean while accusing or else excusing one another;)

16 In the day when God shall judge the secrets of men by Jesus Christ according to my gospel.

Romans 3:19

19 Now we know that what things soever the law saith, it saith to them who are under the law: that every mouth may be stopped, and all the world may become guilty before God.

Matthew 22:36-40

36 Master, which is the great commandment in the law?
37 Jesus said unto him, Thou shalt love the Lord thy God with all thy heart, and with all thy soul, and with all thy mind.
38 This is the first and great commandment.
39 And the second is like unto it, Thou shalt love thy neighbour as thyself.
40 On these two commandments hang all the law and the prophets.

If you love the lord your God with all your heart and with all your soul, and with all your mind and if you love your neighbor as yourself you will not want to do anything against God, and also you will not want to do anything against your neighbor, This is how we fulfill the law.

That is why Jesus said in (Matthew 22:40) On these two commandments hang all the law and the prophets.

And also in (Galations 5:14) further confirms Jesus statement.
Galatians 5:14
14 For all the law is fulfilled in one word, even in this; Thou shalt love thy neighbour as thyself.

Romans 10:8-13

8 But what saith it? The word is nigh thee, even in thy mouth, and in thy heart: that is, the word of faith, which we preach;
9 That if thou shalt confess with thy mouth the Lord Jesus, and shalt believe in thine heart that God hath raised him from the dead, thou shalt be saved.
10 For with the heart man believeth unto righteousness; and with the mouth confession is made unto salvation.
11 For the scripture saith, Whosoever believeth on him shall not be ashamed.
12 For there is no difference between the Jew and the Greek: for the same Lord over all is rich unto all that call upon him.

13 For whosoever shall call upon the name of the Lord shall be saved.

The way we fulfill the law is by doing what jesus said in (Matthew 22:36-40) and also what paul (saul) says in the book of Romans 13:9-10

Romans 13:9-10
9 For this, Thou shalt not commit adultery, Thou shalt not kill, Thou shalt not steal, Thou shalt not bear false witness, Thou shalt not covet; and if there be any other commandment, it is briefly comprehended in this saying, namely, Thou shalt love thy neighbour as thyself.
10 Love worketh no ill to his neighbour: therefore love is the fulfilling of the law.

How God put us right with him.
Romans 3:21-31
21 But now the righteousness of God without the law is manifested, being witnessed by the law and the prophets;
22 Even the righteousness of God which is by faith of Jesus Christ unto all and upon all them that believe: for there is no difference:
23 For all have sinned, and come short of the glory of God;
24 Being justified freely by his grace through the redemption that is in Christ Jesus:
25 Whom God hath set forth to be a propitiation through faith in his blood, to declare his righteousness for the remission of sins that are past, through the forbearance of God;
26 To declare, I say, at this time his righteousness: that he might be just, and the justifier of him which believeth in Jesus.
27 Where is boasting then? It is excluded. By what law? of works? Nay: but by the law of faith.
28 Therefore we conclude that a man is justified by faith without the deeds of the law.
29 Is he the God of the Jews only? is he not also of the Gentiles? Yes, of the Gentiles also:
30 Seeing it is one God, which shall justify the circumcision by faith, and

uncircumcision through faith.

31 Do we then make void the law through faith? God forbid: yea, we establish the law.

Galatians 2:16

16 Knowing that a man is not justified by the works of the law, but by the faith of Jesus Christ, even we have believed in Jesus Christ, that we might be justified by the faith of Christ, and not by the works of the law: for by the works of the law shall no flesh be justified.

Being led by God's spirit.

Romans 8:1-17

1 There is therefore now no condemnation to them which are in Christ Jesus, who walk not after the flesh, but after the Spirit.

2 For the law of the Spirit of life in Christ Jesus hath made me free from the law of sin and death.

3 For what the law could not do, in that it was weak through the flesh, God sending his own Son in the likeness of sinful flesh, and for sin, condemned sin in the flesh:

4 That the righteousness of the law might be fulfilled in us, who walk not after the flesh, but after the Spirit.

5 For they that are after the flesh do mind the things of the flesh; but they that are after the Spirit the things of the Spirit.

6 For to be carnally minded is death; but to be spiritually minded is life and peace.

7 Because the carnal mind is enmity against God: for it is not subject to the law of God, neither indeed can be.

8 So then they that are in the flesh cannot please God.

9 But ye are not in the flesh, but in the Spirit, if so be that the Spirit of God dwell in you. Now if any man have not the Spirit of Christ, he is none of his.

10 And if Christ be in you, the body is dead because of sin; but the Spirit is life because of righteousness.

11 But if the Spirit of him that raised up Jesus from the dead dwell in you,

he that raised up Christ from the dead shall also quicken your mortal bodies by his Spirit that dwelleth in you.

12 Therefore, brethren, we are debtors, not to the flesh, to live after the flesh.

13 For if ye live after the flesh, ye shall die: but if ye through the Spirit do mortify the deeds of the body, ye shall live.

14 For as many as are led by the Spirit of God, they are the sons of God.

15 For ye have not received the spirit of bondage again to fear; but ye have received the Spirit of adoption, whereby we cry, Abba, Father.

16 The Spirit itself beareth witness with our spirit, that we are the children of God:

17 And if children, then heirs; heirs of God, and joint-heirs with Christ; if so be that we suffer with him, that we may be also glorified together.

The fruit of the spirit and the works of the flesh.
Galatians 5:16-26

16 This I say then, Walk in the Spirit, and ye shall not fulfil the lust of the flesh.

17 For the flesh lusteth against the Spirit, and the Spirit against the flesh: and these are contrary the one to the other: so that ye cannot do the things that ye would.

18 But if ye be led of the Spirit, ye are not under the law.

19 Now the works of the flesh are manifest, which are these; Adultery, fornication, uncleanness, lasciviousness,

20 Idolatry, witchcraft, hatred, variance, emulations, wrath, strife, seditions, heresies,

21 Envyings, murders, drunkenness, revellings, and such like: of the which I tell you before, as I have also told you in time past, that they which do such things shall not inherit the kingdom of God.

22 But the fruit of the Spirit is love, joy, peace, longsuffering, gentleness, goodness, faith,

23 Meekness, temperance: against such there is no law.

24 And they that are Christ's have crucified the flesh with the affections and lusts.

25 If we live in the Spirit, let us also walk in the Spirit.
26 Let us not be desirous of vain glory, provoking one another, envying one another.

Galatians 6:21
21 Brethren, if a man be overtaken in a fault, ye which are spiritual, restore such an one in the spirit of meekness; considering thyself, lest thou also be tempted.2 Bear ye one another's burdens, and so fulfil the law of Christ.

The gifts of the Holy Ghost.
1 Corinthians 12:1-11
1 Now concerning spiritual gifts, brethren, I would not have you ignorant.
2 Ye know that ye were Gentiles, carried away unto these dumb idols, even as ye were led.
3 Wherefore I give you to understand, that no man speaking by the Spirit of God calleth Jesus accursed: and that no man can say that Jesus is the Lord, but by the Holy Ghost.
4 Now there are diversities of gifts, but the same Spirit.
5 And there are differences of administrations, but the same Lord.
6 And there are diversities of operations, but it is the same God which worketh all in all.
7 But the manifestation of the Spirit is given to every man to profit withal.
8 For to one is given by the Spirit the word of wisdom; to another the word of knowledge by the same Spirit;
9 To another faith by the same Spirit; to another the gifts of healing by the same Spirit;
10 To another the working of miracles; to another prophecy; to another discerning of spirits; to another divers kinds of tongues; to another the interpretation of tongues:
11 But all these worketh that one and the selfsame Spirit, dividing to every man severally as he will.

The unity of the body.
Ephesians 4:2-16

2 With all lowliness and meekness, with longsuffering, forbearing one another in love;
3 Endeavouring to keep the unity of the Spirit in the bond of peace.
4 There is one body, and one Spirit, even as ye are called in one hope of your calling;
5 One Lord, one faith, one baptism,
6 One God and Father of all, who is above all, and through all, and in you all.
7 But unto every one of us is given grace according to the measure of the gift of Christ.
8 Wherefore he saith, When he ascended up on high, he led captivity captive, and gave gifts unto men.
9 (Now that he ascended, what is it but that he also descended first into the lower parts of the earth?
10 He that descended is the same also that ascended up far above all heavens, that he might fill all things.)
11 And he gave some, apostles; and some, prophets; and some, evangelists; and some, pastors and teachers;
12 For the perfecting of the saints, for the work of the ministry, for the edifying of the body of Christ:
13 Till we all come in the unity of the faith, and of the knowledge of the Son of God, unto a perfect man, unto the measure of the stature of the fulness of Christ:
14 That we henceforth be no more children, tossed to and fro, and carried about with every wind of doctrine, by the sleight of men, and cunning craftiness, whereby they lie in wait to deceive;
15 But speaking the truth in love, may grow up into him in all things, which is the head, even Christ:
16 From whom the whole body fitly joined together and compacted by that which every joint supplieth, according to the effectual working in the measure of every part, maketh increase of the body unto the edifying of itself in love.

Get baptized in the name of The Father, The Son and The Holy Ghost, if

you have not.
Matthew 28:16-20
16 Then the eleven disciples went away into Galilee, into a mountain where Jesus had appointed them.
17 And when they saw him, they worshipped him: but some doubted.
18 And Jesus came and spake unto them, saying, All power is given unto me in heaven and in earth.
19 Go ye therefore, and teach all nations, baptizing them in the name of the Father, and of the Son, and of the Holy Ghost:
20 Teaching them to observe all things whatsoever I have commanded you: and, lo, I am with you always, even unto the end of the world. Amen.

Dead to sin but alive in Jesus the Christ.
Romans 6:1-14
1 What shall we say then? Shall we continue in sin, that grace may abound?
2 God forbid. How shall we, that are dead to sin, live any longer therein?
3 Know ye not, that so many of us as were baptized into Jesus Christ were baptized into his death?
4 Therefore we are buried with him by baptism into death: that like as Christ was raised up from the dead by the glory of the Father, even so we also should walk in newness of life.
5 For if we have been planted together in the likeness of his death, we shall be also in the likeness of his resurrection:
6 Knowing this, that our old man is crucified with him, that the body of sin might be destroyed, that henceforth we should not serve sin.
7 For he that is dead is freed from sin.
8 Now if we be dead with Christ, we believe that we shall also live with him:
9 Knowing that Christ being raised from the dead dieth no more; death hath no more dominion over him.
10 For in that he died, he died unto sin once: but in that he liveth, he liveth unto God.
11 Likewise reckon ye also yourselves to be dead indeed unto sin, but

alive unto God through Jesus Christ our Lord.

12 Let not sin therefore reign in your mortal body, that ye should obey it in the lusts thereof.

13 Neither yield ye your members as instruments of unrighteousness unto sin: but yield yourselves unto God, as those that are alive from the dead, and your members as instruments of righteousness unto God.

14 For sin shall not have dominion over you: for ye are not under the law, but under grace.

Servants of righteousness.
Romans 6:15-23

15 What then? shall we sin, because we are not under the law, but under grace? God forbid.

16 Know ye not, that to whom ye yield yourselves servants to obey, his servants ye are to whom ye obey; whether of sin unto death, or of obedience unto righteousness?

17 But God be thanked, that ye were the servants of sin, but ye have obeyed from the heart that form of doctrine which was delivered you.

18 Being then made free from sin, ye became the servants of righteousness.

19 I speak after the manner of men because of the infirmity of your flesh: for as ye have yielded your members servants to uncleanness and to iniquity unto iniquity; even so now yield your members servants to righteousness unto holiness.

20 For when ye were the servants of sin, ye were free from righteousness.

21 What fruit had ye then in those things whereof ye are now ashamed? for the end of those things is death.

22 But now being made free from sin, and become servants to God, ye have your fruit unto holiness, and the end everlasting life.

23 For the wages of sin is death; but the gift of God is eternal life through Jesus Christ our Lord.

The whole armour of God.
Ephesians 6:10-18

10 Finally, my brethren, be strong in the Lord, and in the power of his might.
11 Put on the whole armour of God, that ye may be able to stand against the wiles of the devil.
12 For we wrestle not against flesh and blood, but against principalities, against powers, against the rulers of the darkness of this world, against spiritual wickedness in high places.
13 Wherefore take unto you the whole armour of God, that ye may be able to withstand in the evil day, and having done all, to stand.
14 Stand therefore, having your loins girt about with truth, and having on the breastplate of righteousness;
15 And your feet shod with the preparation of the gospel of peace;
16 Above all, taking the shield of faith, wherewith ye shall be able to quench all the fiery darts of the wicked.
17 And take the helmet of salvation, and the sword of the Spirit, which is the word of God:
18 Praying always with all prayer and supplication in the Spirit, and watching thereunto with all perseverance and supplication for all saints;

1 Peter 5:8
8 Be sober, be vigilant; because your adversary the devil, as a roaring lion, walketh about, seeking whom he may devour:

Judging othersThe definition of the word Judge: To form an authoritative opinion.
Matthew 7:1-5
1 Judge not, that ye be not judged.
2 For with what judgment ye judge, ye shall be judged: and with what measure ye mete, it shall be measured to you again.
3 And why beholdest thou the mote that is in thy brother's eye, but considerest not the beam that is in thine own eye?
4 Or how wilt thou say to thy brother, Let me pull out the mote out of thine eye; and, behold, a beam is in thine own eye?
5 Thou hypocrite, first cast out the beam out of thine own eye; and then

shalt thou see clearly to cast out the mote out of thy brother's eye.

Looking unto Jesus.
Hebrews 12:1-2
1 Wherefore seeing we also are compassed about with so great a cloud of witnesses, let us lay aside every weight, and the sin which doth so easily beset us, and let us run with patience the race that is set before us,
2 Looking unto Jesus the author and finisher of our faith; who for the joy that was set before him endured the cross, despising the shame, and is set down at the right hand of the throne of God.

Children of God.
1 John 3:1-10
1 Behold, what manner of love the Father hath bestowed upon us, that we should be called the sons of God: therefore the world knoweth us not, because it knew him not.
2 Beloved, now are we the sons of God, and it doth not yet appear what we shall be: but we know that, when he shall appear, we shall be like him; for we shall see him as he is.
3 And every man that hath this hope in him purifieth himself, even as he is pure.
4 Whosoever committeth sin transgresseth also the law: for sin is the transgression of the law.
5 And ye know that he was manifested to take away our sins; and in him is no sin.
6 Whosoever abideth in him sinneth not: whosoever sinneth hath not seen him, neither known him.
7 Little children, let no man deceive you: he that doeth righteousness is righteous, even as he is righteous.
8 He that committeth sin is of the devil; for the devil sinneth from the beginning. For this purpose the Son of God was manifested, that he might destroy the works of the devil.
9 Whosoever is born of God doth not commit sin; for his seed remaineth in him: and he cannot sin, because he is born of God.

10 In this the children of God are manifest, and the children of the devil: whosoever doeth not righteousness is not of God, neither he that loveth not his brother.

Forgive. Matthew 6:14-15

14 For if ye forgive men their trespasses, your heavenly Father will also forgive you:

15 But if ye forgive not men their trespasses, neither will your Father forgive your trespasses.

1 John 1:8-10

8 If we say that we have no sin, we deceive ourselves, and the truth is not in us.

9 If we confess our sins, he is faithful and just to forgive us our sins, and to cleanse us from all unrighteousness.

10 If we say that we have not sinned, we make him a liar, and his word is not in us.

1 John 2:1-2

1 My little children, these things write I unto you, that ye sin not. And if any man sin, we have an advocate with the Father, Jesus Christ the righteous:

2 And he is the propitiation for our sins: and not for ours only, but also for the sins of the whole world.

In union with God.

1 John 2:3-6

3 And hereby we do know that we know him, if we keep his commandments.

4 He that saith, I know him, and keepeth not his commandments, is a liar, and the truth is not in him.

5 But whoso keepeth his word, in him verily is the love of God perfected: hereby know we that we are in him.

6 He that saith he abideth in him ought himself also so to walk, even as he

walked.

Beware of false prophets.
Matthew 7:15-20
15 Beware of false prophets, which come to you in sheep's clothing, but inwardly they are ravening wolves.
16 Ye shall know them by their fruits. Do men gather grapes of thorns, or figs of thistles?
17 Even so every good tree bringeth forth good fruit; but a corrupt tree bringeth forth evil fruit.
18 A good tree cannot bring forth evil fruit, neither can a corrupt tree bring forth good fruit.
19 Every tree that bringeth not forth good fruit is hewn down, and cast into the fire.
20 Wherefore by their fruits ye shall know them.

Endure unto the end.
Luke 21:7-19
7 And they asked him, saying, Master, but when shall these things be? and what sign will there be when these things shall come to pass?
8 And he said, Take heed that ye be not deceived: for many shall come in my name, saying, I am Christ; and the time draweth near: go ye not therefore after them.
9 But when ye shall hear of wars and commotions, be not terrified: for these things must first come to pass; but the end is not by and by.
10 Then said he unto them, Nation shall rise against nation, and kingdom against kingdom:
11 And great earthquakes shall be in divers places, and famines, and pestilences; and fearful sights and great signs shall there be from heaven.
12 But before all these, they shall lay their hands on you, and persecute you, delivering you up to the synagogues, and into prisons, being brought before kings and rulers for my name's sake.
13 And it shall turn to you for a testimony.
14 Settle it therefore in your hearts, not to meditate before what ye shall

answer:

15 For I will give you a mouth and wisdom, which all your adversaries shall not be able to gainsay nor resist.

16 And ye shall be betrayed both by parents, and brethren, and kinsfolks, and friends; and some of you shall they cause to be put to death.

17 And ye shall be hated of all men for my name's sake.

18 But there shall not an hair of your head perish.

19 In your patience possess ye your souls.

Mark 13:13

13 And ye shall be hated of all men for my name's sake: but he that shall endure unto the end, the same shall be saved.

Stay with Jesus the Christ, Endure unto the end and be saved.

Part 4

Running toward the goal.
Philippians 3:12-21

12 Not as though I had already attained, either were already perfect: but I follow after, if that I may apprehend that for which also I am apprehended of Christ Jesus.

13 Brethren, I count not myself to have apprehended: but this one thing I do, forgetting those things which are behind, and reaching forth unto those things which are before,

14 I press toward the mark for the prize of the high calling of God in Christ Jesus.

15 Let us therefore, as many as be perfect, be thus minded: and if in any thing ye be otherwise minded, God shall reveal even this unto you.

16 Nevertheless, whereto we have already attained, let us walk by the same rule, let us mind the same thing.

17 Brethren, be followers together of me, and mark them which walk so as ye have us for an ensample.

18 (For many walk, of whom I have told you often, and now tell you even

weeping, that they are the enemies of the cross of Christ:

19 Whose end is destruction, whose God is their belly, and whose glory is in their shame, who mind earthly things.)

20 For our conversation is in heaven; from whence also we look for the Saviour, the Lord Jesus Christ:

21 Who shall change our vile body, that it may be fashioned like unto his glorious body, according to the working whereby he is able even to subdue all things unto himself.

Gods love in Jesus the Christ.
Romans 8:31-39

31 What shall we then say to these things? If God be for us, who can be against us?

32 He that spared not his own Son, but delivered him up for us all, how shall he not with him also freely give us all things?

33 Who shall lay any thing to the charge of God's elect? It is God that justifieth.

34 Who is he that condemneth? It is Christ that died, yea rather, that is risen again, who is even at the right hand of God, who also maketh intercession for us.

35 Who shall separate us from the love of Christ? shall tribulation, or distress, or persecution, or famine, or nakedness, or peril, or sword?

36 As it is written, For thy sake we are killed all the day long; we are accounted as sheep for the slaughter.

37 Nay, in all these things we are more than conquerors through him that loved us.

38 For I am persuaded, that neither death, nor life, nor angels, nor principalities, nor powers, nor things present, nor things to come,

39 Nor height, nor depth, nor any other creature, shall be able to separate us from the love of God, which is in Christ Jesus our Lord.

Salvation, Quality of work.
1 Corinthians 3:9-15

9 For we are labourers together with God: ye are God's husbandry, ye are

God's building.

10 According to the grace of God which is given unto me, as a wise masterbuilder, I have laid the foundation, and another buildeth thereon. But let every man take heed how he buildeth thereupon.

11 For other foundation can no man lay than that is laid, which is Jesus Christ.

12 Now if any man build upon this foundation gold, silver, precious stones, wood, hay, stubble;

13 Every man's work shall be made manifest: for the day shall declare it, because it shall be revealed by fire; and the fire shall try every man's work of what sort it is.

14 If any man's work abide which he hath built thereupon, he shall receive a reward.

15 If any man's work shall be burned, he shall suffer loss: but he himself shall be saved; yet so as by fire.

Try not to defile the temple of God.
1 Corinthians 3:16-17

16 Know ye not that ye are the temple of God, and that the Spirit of God dwelleth in you?

17 If any man defile the temple of God, him shall God destroy; for the temple of God is holy, which temple ye are.

==========

section - 10 - Some warnings to be aware of.

==========

Some warnings to be aware of.

Please tell your children about the following warnings, It is very important that everyone knows about the warnings, Including family, friends, fellowmen.

Warnings about false Jesus Christs and prophets.
Matthew 24:5

5 For many shall come in my name, saying, I am Christ; and shall deceive

many.

Matthew 24:23-27
23 Then if any man shall say unto you, Lo, here is Christ, or there; believe it not.
24 For there shall arise false Christs, and false prophets, and shall shew great signs and wonders; insomuch that, if it were possible, they shall deceive the very elect.
25 Behold, I have told you before.
26 Wherefore if they shall say unto you, Behold, he is in the desert; go not forth: behold, he is in the secret chambers; believe it not.
27 For as the lightning cometh out of the east, and shineth even unto the west; so shall also the coming of the Son of man be.

Matthew 7:15-20
15 Beware of false prophets, which come to you in sheep's clothing, but inwardly they are ravening wolves.
16 Ye shall know them by their fruits. Do men gather grapes of thorns, or figs of thistles?
17 Even so every good tree bringeth forth good fruit; but a corrupt tree bringeth forth evil fruit.
18 A good tree cannot bring forth evil fruit, neither can a corrupt tree bring forth good fruit.
19 Every tree that bringeth not forth good fruit is hewn down, and cast into the fire.
20 Wherefore by their fruits ye shall know them.

This is just some of the highlites of the book of Revelation, Please read and study the whole book of Revelation.

Tribulation for ten days.
Revelation 2:10-11
10 Fear none of those things which thou shalt suffer: behold, the devil shall cast some of you into prison, that ye may be tried; and ye shall have

tribulation ten days: be thou faithful unto death, and I will give thee a crown of life.
11 He that hath an ear, let him hear what the Spirit saith unto the churches; He that overcometh shall not be hurt of the second death.

Note: The second death is to burn forever in the lake of fire and brimstone.

Scripture probably pointing to a Pre Tribulation Rapture - Resurrection.
Revelation 3:10-13
10 Because thou hast kept the word of my patience, I also will keep thee from the hour of temptation, which shall come upon all the world, to try them that dwell upon the earth.
11 Behold, I come quickly: hold that fast which thou hast, that no man take thy crown.
12 Him that overcometh will I make a pillar in the temple of my God, and he shall go no more out: and I will write upon him the name of my God, and the name of the city of my God, which is new Jerusalem, which cometh down out of heaven from my God: and I will write upon him my new name.
13 He that hath an ear, let him hear what the Spirit saith unto the churches.

Note: You will know that the Pre-Tribulation Rapture - Resurrection is Probably not going to happen or has been missed, If the mark of the beast starts and you are still on the earth. So if you have to die by being beheaded by Gods enemies because you did not accept the mark of the beast or for not worshipping the beast, Die, Because God will raise you back to life one day to reigned with Jesus the Christ a thousand years and I do not know when but you will also receive everlasting life.

Warning concerning the beast and the mark of the beast.
Revelation 13:15-18
15 And he had power to give life unto the image of the beast, that the image of the beast should both speak, and cause that as many as would not worship the image of the beast should be killed.

16 And he causeth all, both small and great, rich and poor, free and bond, to receive a mark in their right hand, or in their foreheads:
17 And that no man might buy or sell, save he that had the mark, or the name of the beast, or the number of his name.
18 Here is wisdom. Let him that hath understanding count the number of the beast: for it is the number of a man; and his number is Six hundred threescore and six.

Another Warning.Revelation 14:9-13
9 And the third angel followed them, saying with a loud voice, If any man worship the beast and his image, and receive his mark in his forehead, or in his hand,
10 The same shall drink of the wine of the wrath of God, which is poured out without mixture into the cup of his indignation; and he shall be tormented with fire and brimstone in the presence of the holy angels, and in the presence of the Lamb:
11 And the smoke of their torment ascendeth up forever and ever: and they have no rest day nor night, who worship the beast and his image, and whosoever receiveth the mark of his name.
12 Here is the patience of the saints: here are they that keep the commandments of God, and the faith of Jesus.
13 And I heard a voice from heaven saying unto me, Write, Blessed are the dead which die in the Lord from henceforth: Yea, saith the Spirit, that they may rest from their labours; and their works do follow them.

Those who got victory and preparing for God the Father wrath. Revelation 15:1-8
1 And I saw another sign in heaven, great and marvellous, seven angels having the seven last plagues; for in them is filled up the wrath of God.
2 And I saw as it were a sea of glass mingled with fire: and them that had gotten the victory over the beast, and over his image, and over his mark, and over the number of his name, stand on the sea of glass, having the harps of God.
3 And they sing the song of Moses the servant of God, and the song of the

Lamb, saying, Great and marvellous are thy works, Lord God Almighty; just and true are thy ways, thou King of saints.

4 Who shall not fear thee, O Lord, and glorify thy name? for thou only art holy: for all nations shall come and worship before thee; for thy judgments are made manifest.

5 And after that I looked, and, behold, the temple of the tabernacle of the testimony in heaven was opened:

6 And the seven angels came out of the temple, having the seven plagues, clothed in pure and white linen, and having their breasts girded with golden girdles.

7 And one of the four beasts gave unto the seven angels seven golden vials full of the wrath of God, who liveth for ever and ever.

8 And the temple was filled with smoke from the glory of God, and from his power; and no man was able to enter into the temple, till the seven plagues of the seven angels were fulfilled.

The pouring of the vials, What will be happening during the time of the mark of the beast.

Revelation 16:1-21

1 And I heard a great voice out of the temple saying to the seven angels, Go your ways, and pour out the vials of the wrath of God upon the earth.

2 And the first went, and poured out his vial upon the earth; and there fell a noisome and grievous sore upon the men which had the mark of the beast, and upon them which worshipped his image.

3 And the second angel poured out his vial upon the sea; and it became as the blood of a dead man: and every living soul died in the sea.

4 And the third angel poured out his vial upon the rivers and fountains of waters; and they became blood.

5 And I heard the angel of the waters say, Thou art righteous, O Lord, which art, and wast, and shalt be, because thou hast judged thus.

6 For they have shed the blood of saints and prophets, and thou hast given them blood to drink; for they are worthy.

7 And I heard another out of the altar say, Even so, Lord God Almighty, true and righteous are thy judgments.

8 And the fourth angel poured out his vial upon the sun; and power was given unto him to scorch men with fire.
9 And men were scorched with great heat, and blasphemed the name of God, which hath power over these plagues: and they repented not to give him glory.
10 And the fifth angel poured out his vial upon the seat of the beast; and his kingdom was full of darkness; and they gnawed their tongues for pain,
11 And blasphemed the God of heaven because of their pains and their sores, and repented not of their deeds.
12 And the sixth angel poured out his vial upon the great river Euphrates; and the water thereof was dried up, that the way of the kings of the east might be prepared.
13 And I saw three unclean spirits like frogs come out of the mouth of the dragon, and out of the mouth of the beast, and out of the mouth of the false prophet.
14 For they are the spirits of devils, working miracles, which go forth unto the kings of the earth and of the whole world, to gather them to the battle of that great day of God Almighty.
15 Behold, I come as a thief. Blessed is he that watcheth, and keepeth his garments, lest he walk naked, and they see his shame.
16 And he gathered them together into a place called in the Hebrew tongue Armageddon.
17 And the seventh angel poured out his vial into the air; and there came a great voice out of the temple of heaven, from the throne, saying, It is done.
18 And there were voices, and thunders, and lightnings; and there was a great earthquake, such as was not since men were upon the earth, so mighty an earthquake, and so great.
19 And the great city was divided into three parts, and the cities of the nations fell: and great Babylon came in remembrance before God, to give unto her the cup of the wine of the fierceness of his wrath.
20 And every island fled away, and the mountains were not found.
21 And there fell upon men a great hail out of heaven, every stone about the weight of a talent: and men blasphemed God because of the plague of the hail; for the plague thereof was exceeding great.

Jesus and his armies.
Revelation 19:1-21

1 And after these things I heard a great voice of much people in heaven, saying, Alleluia; Salvation, and glory, and honour, and power, unto the Lord our God:

2 For true and righteous are his judgments: for he hath judged the great whore, which did corrupt the earth with her fornication, and hath avenged the blood of his servants at her hand.

3 And again they said, Alleluia And her smoke rose up for ever and ever.

4 And the four and twenty elders and the four beasts fell down and worshipped God that sat on the throne, saying, Amen; Alleluia.

5 And a voice came out of the throne, saying, Praise our God, all ye his servants, and ye that fear him, both small and great.

6 And I heard as it were the voice of a great multitude, and as the voice of many waters, and as the voice of mighty thunderings, saying, Alleluia: for the Lord God omnipotent reigneth.

7 Let us be glad and rejoice, and give honour to him: for the marriage of the Lamb is come, and his wife hath made herself ready.

8 And to her was granted that she should be arrayed in fine linen, clean and white: for the fine linen is the righteousness of saints.

9 And he saith unto me, Write, Blessed are they which are called unto the marriage supper of the Lamb. And he saith unto me, These are the true sayings of God.

10 And I fell at his feet to worship him. And he said unto me, See thou do it not: I am thy fellowservant, and of thy brethren that have the testimony of Jesus: worship God: for the testimony of Jesus is the spirit of prophecy.

11 And I saw heaven opened, and behold a white horse; and he that sat upon him was called Faithful and True, and in righteousness he doth judge and make war.

12 His eyes were as a flame of fire, and on his head were many crowns; and he had a name written, that no man knew, but he himself.

13 And he was clothed with a vesture dipped in blood: and his name is called The Word of God.

14 And the armies which were in heaven followed him upon white horses, clothed in fine linen, white and clean.

15 And out of his mouth goeth a sharp sword, that with it he should smite the nations: and he shall rule them with a rod of iron: and he treadeth the winepress of the fierceness and wrath of Almighty God.

16 And he hath on his vesture and on his thigh a name written, King Of Kings, And Lord Of Lords.

17 And I saw an angel standing in the sun; and he cried with a loud voice, saying to all the fowls that fly in the midst of heaven, Come and gather yourselves together unto the supper of the great God;

18 That ye may eat the flesh of kings, and the flesh of captains, and the flesh of mighty men, and the flesh of horses, and of them that sit on them, and the flesh of all men, both free and bond, both small and great.

19 And I saw the beast, and the kings of the earth, and their armies, gathered together to make war against him that sat on the horse, and against his army.

20 And the beast was taken, and with him the false prophet that wrought miracles before him, with which he deceived them that had received the mark of the beast, and them that worshipped his image. These both were cast alive into a lake of fire burning with brimstone.

21 And the remnant were slain with the sword of him that sat upon the horse, which sword proceeded out of his mouth: and all the fowls were filled with their flesh.

Blessings for those who die by being beheaded. - The first Rapture - Resurrection.
Revelation 20:4-6

4 And I saw thrones, and they sat upon them, and judgment was given unto them: and I saw the souls of them that were beheaded for the witness of Jesus, and for the word of God, and which had not worshipped the beast, neither his image, neither had received his mark upon their foreheads, or in their hands; and they lived and reigned with Christ a thousand years.

5 But the rest of the dead lived not again until the thousand years were finished. This is the first resurrection.

6 Blessed and holy is he that hath part in the first resurrection: on such the second death hath no power, but they shall be priests of God and of Christ, and shall reign with him a thousand years.

Note: The second death has no power because they have eternal life.

Reminder: you will know that it is the mark of the beast because you will not be able to buy or sell without it, Do not get it for any reason.

Pray that everyone be warned about the mark of the beast and what it is.
The prayer.
Father God in heaven, please warn more people about the mark of the beast and what it is.   This I humbly ask in Jesus the Christ Holy name, amen.

Note: I strongly believe that one of the mark of the beast might be an RFID microchip about the size of a grain of rice or it might be smaller, If you are told by a financial institution that you need one to buy and sell or if your doctor try to give you one to keep track of medical records or to confirm that you received a vaccine or your Job, school or church try to give you one, Please don't get one for any reason.

Even if it means dying by being beheaded by God the Father enemies.

Loveing and fearing God the Father enough to die for him just as Jesus did.

Loveing God the Father.
Matthew 22:36-38
36 Master, which is the great commandment in the law?
37 Jesus said unto him, Thou shalt love the Lord thy God with all thy heart, and with all thy soul, and with all thy mind.
38 This is the first and great commandment.

Fearing God the Father. Matthew 10:28
28 And fear not them which kill the body, but are not able to kill the soul: but rather fear him which is able to destroy both soul and body in hell.

Reminder: I just touched on some of the highlites of the book of Revelation, Please read and study the whole book of Revelation.

Again, Please tell your children about the warnings, It is very important that everyone knows about the warnings, Including Family, Friends and our Fellowmen.

Look to Jesus just like I am, because there is only salvation in him.

Please read and study the Holy Bible.   Take it seriously.   May God the Father bless you.   And I hope to see you in the new heaven and the new earth to come.   Aman.

Please do not get a AI mind chip implant in your brain. It is very dangerous to do this, such as, it might get a virus or it may be used to control you or urge you to take the mark of the beast, etc. we have been doing just fine all this time without one. when God the Father and Jesus the Christ come and visit us. It is in the brain and the Holy Spirit lives there all the time. Please leave it as natural as possible. especially if you are a Christian, I will resist to the death, before I would get one and so should everybody.

Please do not get a humanoid robot. I tell you this, for your own good. Please do not do it.

It is safer to read the Holy Bible, Do not listen to the Holy Bible on the internet, cassette tapes, mp3, etc.

Please throw away or delete your audio files, This is truly, honestly the best for you, These audio files are truly dangerous, Because it talks about good and bad forces, and they might effect you in a good way. and in a bad way. Just read it to yourself and out loud to each other.

When you read your Holy Bible, you should pray to God the Father over the Holy Bible, that you are protected by him.

If you do listen to the Holy Bible on the internet, cassette tapes, mp3, etc. Listen for short periods at a time and before you start, pray to God the Father that you are protected from bad forces, asking in Jesus the Christ name, God The Father will do this for you.

If you feel that you have sinned in a big way, I encourage you again to continue your Christian walk anyway for salvation.

One of the things the devil (Gods enemy) does is try to make you think that things are more worse than they really are, and it's just not.

If you left, for any reason, return to Jesus the Christ (The sent one) and be healed in every way.
Living a loving life is the answer. Live your loving life.

    Pray that people return to God the Father, Jesus Christ and the Holy Spirit.

The prayer
    God the Father, Please guide the people back to you who left, this I humbly ask in Jesus Holy name. Aman

Please tell others about Jesus the Christ (The sent one).
Revelation 22:16-17
16 "I, Jesus, have sent my angel to give you[a] this testimony for the churches. I am the Root and the Offspring of David, and the bright Morning Star."
17 The Spirit and the bride say, "Come!" And let the one who hears say,

"Come!" Let the one who is thirsty come; and let the one who wishes take the free gift of the water of life.
Again: Look to Jesus just like I am, because there is only salvation in him.

Repenting of sins.   Saving others is saving yourself.
James 5:19-20
19 My brothers and sisters, if one of you should wander from the truth and someone should bring that person back,
20 remember this: Whoever turns a sinner from the error of their way will save them from death and cover over a multitude of sins.

Please tell peole about this booklet.

I ask that only Christians pray for the people on the list, thank you.

About Prayer.
James 5:16
Therefore confess your sins to each other and pray for each other so that you may be healed. The prayer of a righteous person is powerful and effective.

About petitions, prayers, intercession.
1 Timothy 2:1-3
1 I urge, then, first of all, that petitions, prayers, intercession and thanksgiving be made for all people
2 for kings and all those in authority, that we may live peaceful and quiet lives in all godliness and holiness.
3 This is good, and pleases God our Savior,

Share with your fellow men and loved ones and if you can, E-mail a copy to them.

It is about being ready for Jesus the Christ soon return.

Use this booklet to examine your self to see if you are in God the Father will, If you start doubting yourself, come back to this book to see if there is any changes you need to make to your life.

Before you get married, have your fiance read this booklet and agree to live by it.

===========

Section - 11 - Forgiveness for blasphemy of the Holy Ghost.

This added section is good news, to the Jewish people and everyone else, a lot of people would not be saved if it was not for this provision in the Holy Bible.
===========

Note: The Holy Ghost is also known as the Holy Spirit.

"Forgiveness for blasphemy of the Holy Ghost."

Blasphemy: Occurs when a person speaks against God, Jesus, Holy Ghost or another person offensively.

Is there forgiveness for the unpardonable eternal sin Jesus is speaking about in Mark 3:28-29?

What Jesus said before God and him started forgiving Blasphemy against the Holy Spirit.

Mark 3:28-29
28 Verily I say unto you, All sins shall be forgiven unto the

sons of men, and blasphemies wherewith soever they shall blaspheme:

29 But he that shall blaspheme against the Holy Ghost hath never forgiveness, but is in danger of eternal damnation.

The answer is yes. Blasphemy against God, Jesus and the Holy Spirit is forgivable whether it is on purpose or not. God and Jesus wanted to save the people that blasphemed the Holy Ghost, Jesus accomplished this by calling and saving Saul (Paul).

Paul before he accepted Jesus.
Acts 26:9-11
9 "I too was convinced that I ought to do all that was possible to oppose the name of Jesus of Nazareth.
10 And that is just what I did in Jerusalem. On the authority of the chief priests I put many of the Lord's people in prison, and when they were put to death, I cast my vote against them.
11 Many a time I went from one synagogue to another to have them punished, and I tried to force them to blaspheme. I was so obsessed with persecuting them that I even hunted them down in foreign cities.

I Timothy 1:13
13 Even though I was once a blasphemer and a persecutor and a violent man, I was shown mercy because I acted in ignorance and unbelief.

Paul being called and saved by Jesus.
Acts 9:1-18
1 And Saul, yet breathing out threatenings and slaughter against the disciples of the Lord, went unto the high priest,
2 And desired of him letters to Damascus to the synagogues,

that if he found any of this way, whether they were men or women, he might bring them bound unto Jerusalem.

3 And as he journeyed, he came near Damascus: and suddenly there shined round about him a light from heaven:

4 And he fell to the earth, and heard a voice saying unto him, Saul, Saul, why persecutest thou me?

5 And he said, Who art thou, Lord? And the Lord said, I am Jesus whom thou persecutest: it is hard for thee to kick against the pricks.

6 And he trembling and astonished said, Lord, what wilt thou have me to do? And the Lord said unto him, Arise, and go into the city, and it shall be told thee what thou must do.

7 And the men which journeyed with him stood speechless, hearing a voice, but seeing no man.

8 And Saul arose from the earth; and when his eyes were opened, he saw no man: but they led him by the hand, and brought him into Damascus.

9 And he was three days without sight, and neither did eat nor drink.

10 And there was a certain disciple at Damascus, named Ananias; and to him said the Lord in a vision, Ananias. And he said, Behold, I am here, Lord.

11 And the Lord said unto him, Arise, and go into the street which is called Straight, and enquire in the house of Judas for one called Saul, of Tarsus: for, behold, he prayeth,

12 And hath seen in a vision a man named Ananias coming in, and putting his hand on him, that he might receive his sight.

13 Then Ananias answered, Lord, I have heard by many of this man, how much evil he hath done to thy saints at Jerusalem:

14 And here he hath authority from the chief priests to bind all that call on thy name.

15 But the Lord said unto him, Go thy way: for he is a chosen vessel unto me, to bear my name before the Gentiles, and kings, and the children of Israel:

16 For I will shew him how great things he must suffer for my name's sake.

17 And Ananias went his way, and entered into the house; and putting his hands on him said, Brother Saul, the Lord, even Jesus, that appeared unto thee in the way as thou camest, hath sent me, that thou mightest receive thy sight, and be filled with the Holy Ghost.

18 And immediately there fell from his eyes as it had been scales: and he received sight forthwith, and arose, and was baptized.

   Note: The reason why it was Jesus the Christ that blinded Paul and not Satan (Devil), Is because nowhere in the Holy Bible does it say satan has that ability nor does Satan shows that ability in the Holy Bible.

   God the Father, Jesus the Christ and and Holy Angels on the other hand demonstrate that they have the ability to affect people eyes, and it is all through the Holy Bible, This is how You know that it was Jesus the Christ and not Satan that talked to and blinded Paul (saul), Now he see's just fine because his sight was restored.

Forgivable sin
Concerning I Timothy 1:13, 13
13 Even though I was once a blasphemer and a persecutor and a violent man, I was shown mercy because I acted in ignorance and unbelief.

Paul was not forgiven because he persecuted Christians and blasphemed in ignorance.

Jesus mentions nothing about doing something in ignorance, Jesus forgave Paul because he wanted to and in doing so anyone who blasphemes the Holy Ghost by accident or on purpose can be forgiven and saved.

This is one of the things that was accomplished when Jesus called and saved Paul.

Another example where God the Father changed his mind.
Jonah 3:10

10 And God saw their works, that they turned from their evil way; and God repented of the evil, that he had said that he would do unto them; and he did it not.

Another example of comming back to God the Father in the

parable Jesus tells.
Luke 15:1-32
1 Then drew near unto him all the publicans and sinners for to hear him.
2 And the Pharisees and scribes murmured, saying, This man receiveth sinners, and eateth with them.
3 And he spake this parable unto them, saying,
4 What man of you, having an hundred sheep, if he lose one of them, doth not leave the ninety and nine in the wilderness, and go after that which is lost, until he find it?
5 And when he hath found it, he layeth it on his shoulders, rejoicing.
6 And when he cometh home, he calleth together his friends and neighbours, saying unto them, Rejoice with me; for I have

found my sheep which was lost.

7 I say unto you, that likewise joy shall be in heaven over one sinner that repenteth, more than over ninety and nine just persons, which need no repentance.

8 Either what woman having ten pieces of silver, if she lose one piece, doth not light a candle, and sweep the house, and seek diligently till she find it?

9 And when she hath found it, she calleth her friends and her neighbours together, saying, Rejoice with me; for I have found the piece which I had lost.

10 Likewise, I say unto you, there is joy in the presence of the angels of God over one sinner that repenteth.

11 And he said, A certain man had two sons:

12 And the younger of them said to his father, Father, give me the portion of goods that falleth to me. And he divided unto them his living.

13 And not many days after the younger son gathered all together, and took his journey into a far country, and there wasted his substance with riotous living.

14 And when he had spent all, there arose a mighty famine in that land; and he began to be in want.

15 And he went and joined himself to a citizen of that country; and he sent him into his fields to feed swine.

16 And he would fain have filled his belly with the husks that the swine did eat: and no man gave unto him.

17 And when he came to himself, he said, How many hired servants of my father's have bread enough and to spare, and I perish with hunger!

18 I will arise and go to my father, and will say unto him, Father, I have sinned against heaven, and before thee,

19 And am no more worthy to be called thy son: make me as one of thy hired servants.

20 And he arose, and came to his father. But when he was yet

a great way off, his father saw him, and had compassion, and ran, and fell on his neck, and kissed him.

21 And the son said unto him, Father, I have sinned against heaven, and in thy sight, and am no more worthy to be called thy son.

22 But the father said to his servants, Bring forth the best robe, and put it on him; and put a ring on his hand, and shoes on his feet:

23 And bring hither the fatted calf, and kill it; and let us eat, and be merry:

24 For this my son was dead, and is alive again; he was lost, and is found. And they began to be merry.

25 Now his elder son was in the field: and as he came and drew nigh to the house, he heard music and dancing.

26 And he called one of the servants, and asked what these things meant.

27 And he said unto him, Thy brother is come; and thy father hath killed the fatted calf, because he hath received him safe and sound.

28 And he was angry, and would not go in: therefore came his father out, and intreated him.

29 And he answering said to his father, Lo, these many years do I serve thee, neither transgressed I at any time thy commandment: and yet thou never gavest me a kid, that I might make merry with my friends:

30 But as soon as this thy son was come, which hath devoured thy living with harlots, thou hast killed for him the fatted calf.

31 And he said unto him, Son, thou art ever with me, and all that I have is thine.

32 It was meet that we should make merry, and be glad: for this thy brother was dead, and is alive again; and was lost, and is found.

Thanks for reading, please share this information, one way is to

E-mail this information to family and friends and strangers, or have a Holy bible study, etc.

If you would like a hard copy, Go to Amazon.com, Type this book tittled: Urgent, Need to know information, For Christians and non Christians.
===========
Heaven is a gift from God the Father to the saved of mankind.
Strive for it.
===========

Living a Loving Life.

The cost of living a loving life for God the Father, Jesus the Christ and the Holy Sprit.

The cost may be letting your loved ones and friends not be written in the book of life, if that is what they want, talk to them, pray for them, that they come to there senses and escape the trap that satan the devil has set.

The fact is that not everyone is going to be saved. I do not like it but that is just the way it is.

We may have to die for God the Father, Jesus the Christ and the Holy Spirit.

Jesus died for us, so we can get forgiven for our sins, we may have to die for God the Father, Jesus the Christ and the Holy Sprit, to be faithful to the death to prove our faith in them.

That may be the cost of loving them, that is just the way it is.

We are in a battle of good against evil, good must win at all cost, because God the Father, Jesus the Christ and the Holy Sprit only wants the best for mankind; satan the devil. only wants you to burn forever with him, in the lake of fire and brimstone.

God the Father destroyed everyone on earth with the great flood because of sins, except for eight people, on noah's ark, that is how serious this battle is, next time it will be by fire and brimstone.

Put God the Father, Jesus the Christ and the Holy Sprit, first in your life; you must do this to survive here on earth and hopefully later in heaven, If you make it to the new heaven and the new earth, you should be safe.

Live your life of love.

Be brave to the end to be saved and receive everlasting life.

Revelation 21:1-27
1 And I saw a new heaven and a new earth: for the first heaven and the first earth were passed away; and there was no more sea.
2 And I John saw the holy city, new Jerusalem, coming down from God out of heaven, prepared as a bride adorned for her husband.
3 And I heard a great voice out of heaven saying, Behold, the tabernacle of God is with men, and he will dwell with them, and they shall be his people, and God himself shall be with them, and be their God.
4 And God shall wipe away all tears from their eyes; and there shall be no more death, neither sorrow, nor crying, neither shall there be any more pain: for the former things are passed away.
5 And he that sat upon the throne said, Behold, I make all things new. And he said unto me, Write: for these words are true and faithful.
6 And he said unto me, It is done. I am Alpha and Omega, the beginning and the end. I will give unto him that is athirst of the fountain of the water of life freely.
7 He that overcometh shall inherit all things; and I will be his God, and he shall be my son.
8 But the fearful, and unbelieving, and the abominable, and murderers, and whoremongers, and sorcerers, and idolaters, and all liars, shall have their part in the lake which burneth with fire and brimstone: which is the second

death.

9 And there came unto me one of the seven angels which had the seven vials full of the seven last plagues, and talked with me, saying, Come hither, I will shew thee the bride, the Lamb's wife.

10 And he carried me away in the spirit to a great and high mountain, and shewed me that great city, the holy Jerusalem, descending out of heaven from God,

11 Having the glory of God: and her light was like unto a stone most precious, even like a jasper stone, clear as crystal;

12 And had a wall great and high, and had twelve gates, and at the gates twelve angels, and names written thereon, which are the names of the twelve tribes of the children of Israel:

13 On the east three gates; on the north three gates; on the south three gates; and on the west three gates.

14 And the wall of the city had twelve foundations, and in them the names of the twelve apostles of the Lamb.

15 And he that talked with me had a golden reed to measure the city, and the gates thereof, and the wall thereof.

16 And the city lieth foursquare, and the length is as large as the breadth: and he measured the city with the reed, twelve thousand furlongs. The length and the breadth and the height of it are equal.

17 And he measured the wall thereof, an hundred and forty and four cubits, according to the measure of a man, that is, of the angel.

18 And the building of the wall of it was of jasper: and the city was pure gold, like unto clear glass.

19 And the foundations of the wall of the city were garnished with all manner of precious stones. The first foundation was jasper; the second, sapphire; the third, a chalcedony; the fourth, an emerald;

20 The fifth, sardonyx; the sixth, sardius; the seventh, chrysolyte; the eighth, beryl; the ninth, a topaz; the tenth, a chrysoprasus; the eleventh, a jacinth; the twelfth, an amethyst.

21 And the twelve gates were twelve pearls: every several gate was of one pearl: and the street of the city was pure gold, as it were transparent glass.

22 And I saw no temple therein: for the Lord God Almighty and the Lamb

are the temple of it.

23 And the city had no need of the sun, neither of the moon, to shine in it: for the glory of God did lighten it, and the Lamb is the light thereof.

24 And the nations of them which are saved shall walk in the light of it: and the kings of the earth do bring their glory and honour into it.

25 And the gates of it shall not be shut at all by day: for there shall be no night there.

26 And they shall bring the glory and honour of the nations into it.

27 And there shall in no wise enter into it any thing that defileth, neither whatsoever worketh abomination, or maketh a lie: but they which are written in the Lamb's book of life.

Revelation 22:1-21

1 And he shewed me a pure river of water of life, clear as crystal, proceeding out of the throne of God and of the Lamb.

2 In the midst of the street of it, and on either side of the river, was there the tree of life, which bare twelve manner of fruits, and yielded her fruit every month: and the leaves of the tree were for the healing of the nations.

3 And there shall be no more curse: but the throne of God and of the Lamb shall be in it; and his servants shall serve him:

4 And they shall see his face; and his name shall be in their foreheads.

5 And there shall be no night there; and they need no candle, neither light of the sun; for the Lord God giveth them light: and they shall reign for ever and ever.

6 And he said unto me, These sayings are faithful and true: and the Lord God of the holy prophets sent his angel to shew unto his servants the things which must shortly be done.

7 Behold, I come quickly: blessed is he that keepeth the sayings of the prophecy of this book.

8 And I John saw these things, and heard them. And when I had heard and seen, I fell down to worship before the feet of the angel which shewed me these things.

9 Then saith he unto me, See thou do it not: for I am thy fellowservant, and of thy brethren the prophets, and of them which keep the sayings of this

book: worship God.

10 And he saith unto me, Seal not the sayings of the prophecy of this book: for the time is at hand.

11 He that is unjust, let him be unjust still: and he which is filthy, let him be filthy still: and he that is righteous, let him be righteous still: and he that is holy, let him be holy still.

12 And, behold, I come quickly; and my reward is with me, to give every man according as his work shall be.

13 I am Alpha and Omega, the beginning and the end, the first and the last.

14 Blessed are they that do his commandments, that they may have right to the tree of life, and may enter in through the gates into the city.

15 For without are dogs, and sorcerers, and whoremongers, and murderers, and idolaters, and whosoever loveth and maketh a lie.

16 I Jesus have sent mine angel to testify unto you these things in the churches. I am the root and the offspring of David, and the bright and morning star.

17 And the Spirit and the bride say, Come. And let him that heareth say, Come. And let him that is athirst come. And whosoever will, let him take the water of life freely.

18 For I testify unto every man that heareth the words of the prophecy of this book, If any man shall add unto these things, God shall add unto him the plagues that are written in this book:

19 And if any man shall take away from the words of the book of this prophecy, God shall take away his part out of the book of life, and out of the holy city, and from the things which are written in this book.

20 He which testifieth these things saith, Surely I come quickly. Amen. Even so, come, Lord Jesus.

21 The grace of our Lord Jesus Christ be with you all. Amen.

===========

Read and study the Holy Bible.

===========

This booklet is dedicated to God the Father, Jesus the Christ, the Holy Spirit and the saved ones, amen.

===========

I say this to my fellowmen, strive to be a saved one.

==========

Last note: Talk to God the Father, Jesus the Christ and the Holy Spirit, with respect, dignity, kindness and reverence, They are our creators, family and our friends.

==========

Pray to God the Father for the second coming of Jesus the Christ, asking him in Jesus the Christ name.

==========

Matthew 18:19-20

19 Again I say unto you, That if two of you shall agree on earth as touching any thing that they shall ask, it shall be done for them of my Father which is in heaven.

20 For where two or three are gathered together in my name, there am I in the midst of them.

==========

Romans 12:1-3

1 I beseech you therefore, brethren, by the mercies of God, that ye present your bodies a living sacrifice, holy, acceptable unto God, which is your reasonable service.

2 And be not conformed to this world: but be ye transformed by the renewing of your mind, that ye may prove what is that good, and acceptable, and perfect, will of God.

3 For I say, through the grace given unto me, to every man that is among you, not to think of himself more highly than he ought to think; but to think soberly, according as God hath dealt to every man the measure of faith.

==========

It is done.